TWAYNE'S WORLD AUTHORS SERIES
A Survey of the World's Literature

DENMARK

Leif Sjöberg
State University of New York at Stony Brook

EDITOR

Vilhelm Grønbech

TWAS 397

Vilhelm Grønbech

VILHELM GRØNBECH

By P. M. MITCHELL
University of Illinois at Urbana-Champaign

ST. JOSEPH'S UNIVERSITY   STX

BL43.G76M57   Vilhelm Grønbech /

3 9353 00116 9067

226876

BL
43
.G76
M57

TWAYNE PUBLISHERS
A DIVISION OF G. K. HALL & CO., BOSTON

Copyright © 1978 G. K. Hall & Co.
All Rights Reserved
First Printing

Library of Congress Cataloging in Publication Data

Mitchell, Phillip Marshall, 1916–
  Vilhelm Grønbech.

  (Twayne's world authors series ; TWAS 397)
  Bibliography: p. 157–59.
  Includes index.
  1. Grønbech, Vilhelm Peter, 1873–1948.
BL43.G76M57   200'.92'4 [B]   77-8272
ISBN 0-8057-6306-6

MANUFACTURED IN THE UNITED STATES OF AMERICA

Contents

About the Author

P. M. Mitchell received the Ph.D. degree from the University of Illinois in 1942. He has been a professor in the Department of Germanic Languages at the University of Illinois since 1958. He has taught previously at Cornell University, Harvard University, and the University of Kansas. He has been a guest professor at the University of Wisconsin and the University of Aarhus.

Professor Mitchell's publications include: *A Bibliographical Guide to Danish Literature* (1951); *Selected Essays of Ludvig Holberg*, translated, with an Introduction and Notes (1955); *A History of Danish Literature*, with an introductory chapter by Mogens Haugsted (Copenhagen, 1957; 2nd, augmented edition, 1971); *A Bibliography of English Imprints of Denmark* (1960); Vilhelm Grønbech, *Religious Currents in the Nineteenth Century*, translated from the Danish (with W. D. Paden) (1964); *A Bibliography of 17th Century German Imprints of Denmark and the Duchies of Schleswig-Holstein* I–II (1969); III (1976); *Vilhelm Grønbech. En Indføring* (1970); *Anthology of Danish Literature*, bilingual edition, edited with F. J. Billeskov Jansen (1971); *Bibliography of Modern Icelandic Literature in Translation* (with Kenneth H. Ober) (1975).

Professor Mitchell has served as co-editor of the *Journal of English and Germanic Philology* since 1959.

Preface

No assessment of modern Danish culture—religious, literary, or philosophical—is possible without a consideration of Vilhelm Grøn-bech, the outstanding thinker that Denmark has produced in the twentieth century. He was a distinguished scholar of the history of religion for forty years. In the 1930s and 1940s he became a source of inspiration and stimulus for a generation oppressed by political unrest and war.

The present volume attempts to describe and evaluate Grøn-bech's major historical, critical, and interpretive works and also to identify the recurrent ideas that inform them. Grønbech's poetry and novels are mentioned only in passing, for they have had no impact on the reading public; that Grønbech was a master of language and an imaginative writer is easily demonstrable in his other works. No one who has read one of Grønbech's books has remained unimpressed by it; no one who heard Grønbech speak has forgotten the experience.

My own views of Grønbech have developed from a long-time concern with his works as well as from conversations with some of Grønbech's relatives, students, and acquaintances, to all of whom I am indebted for information and helpful ideas. Their opinions often differed widely and are not always reflected in the conclusions that I have drawn.

P. M. MITCHELL

University of Illinois

Chronology

1873 14 June: Vilhelm Peter Grønbech born in Allinge on the island of Bornholm.

1890 Enters the University of Copenhagen.

1897 Receives the degree of "cand[idatus] mag[isterii]"

1896– Teaches in various schools in Copenhagen.
1906

1899– Works part time in the Royal Library.
1900

1902 Defends his dissertation, *Forstudier til tyrkisk lydhistorie (An Introduction to the Study of Turkish Phonetics)*. Receives dr. phil. degree.

1902– Functions as organist at St. Jacob's Church in Copenhagen.
1906

1903 Publishes a volume of poems, *Morituri*.

1903– Lectures at the University of Copenhagen as an unsalaried
1908 *privatdocent*.

1905 Publishes a vocabulary on the dialect of Bokhara.

1908– Teaches English language and literature at the university.
1911

1909 Publishes volume I of *Vor Folkeæt i Oldtiden (The Culture of the Teutons)*.

1911 Appointed *docent* in the history of religion at the university.

1912 Publishes volumes II, III, and IV of *Vor Folkeæt i Oldtiden (The Culture of the Teutons)*.

1913 *Religionsskiftet i Norden (The Conversion of the North)*.

1914 Refuses a call to the University of Leipzig.

1915 *Primitiv religion (Primitive Religion)* published in Stockholm. Grønbech appointed professor of the history of religion at the University of Copenhagen.

1922 *Religiøse strømninger i det nittende aarhundrede (Religious Currents of the Nineteenth Century)*.

1925 Volume I of *Mystikere i Europa og Indien (Mystics in Europe and India)*.

1926 A retelling of Scandinavian myths and tales first published in Stockholm as *Nordiska myter och sagor*. Published the next year in Danish as *Nordiske Myter og Sagn*.

1930 Volume of essays, *Kampen om mennesket (The Struggle for the Human Being)*.
1932 Volume II of *Mystikere i Europa og Indien*, dealing with Heraklitus, Meister Eckehart, and Ruysbroek. Volume III of *Mystikere i Europa og Indien*, dealing with Teresa de Jesus.
1933 *William Blake*.
1934 Volume IV of *Mystikere i Europa og Indien*, dealing with Donne, Wordsworth, and Herder.
1935 *Jesus, menneskesønnen (Jesus, the Son of Man); Goethe I; Friedrich Schlegel i årene 1791–1808 (Friedrich Schlegel in the years 1791–1808)*.
1940 *Hellenismen* I–II; *Sejersen fra Variager (Sejersen from Variager)*, a novel; collection of essays entitled *Kampen för en ny själ (The Struggle for a New Soul)* published in Stockholm, a partial Danish translation issued in 1946 under the title *Kampen for en ny sjæl; Paulus*.
1941 *Solen har mange veje (The Sun Has Many Paths)*, a collection of poems; *Kristus*.
1942 *Hellas* I–II.
1943 *Sprogets musik (The Music of Language)*; 28 May: Grønbech gives his farewell lecture at the university.
1944 *Hellas* IV; *Sangen om livet og døden (The Song of Life and Death)*, a collection of poems; *Vorherre på bjerget (Our Lord on the Mountain)*, a collection of poems.
1945 *Hellas* III.
1946 *Madonna og gøgleren (The Madonna and the Juggler)*, a novel.
1946– *Frie Ord (Free Words)*, a periodical edited by Vilhelm
1948 Grønbech and Hal Koch.
1948 21 April: Grønbech dies.

CHAPTER 1

Introduction

WITH its small and homogeneous population, Denmark has during the last two and a half centuries time and again produced outstanding writers and thinkers who have helped stimulate men's imaginations and mold men's minds both at home and abroad. To the names of the Norwegian-born dramatist and essayist Ludvig Holberg, the incomparable storytellers Hans Christian Andersen and Karen Blixen, the religious philosopher Søren Kierkegaard, the physicists Hans Christian Ørsted and Niels Bohr, and the critic Georg Brandes—to mention some particularly well-known figures—should be added that of Vilhelm Grønbech, an outstanding historian of religion, an incisive analyst, and a synthetic thinker who has exerted a pervasive influence on his own countrymen and who occupies a central position within Danish culture in the first half of the twentieth century, although his impact outside Denmark has been sparse and scattered.

One cannot consider the history of religion, philosophy, or literature in twentieth century Scandinavia without including Vilhelm Grønbech, who, although in the first instance neither a religious leader nor a philosopher nor a poet or novelist, addressed himself critically and incisively to religious and philosophical matters and shared several characteristics with poets and imaginative writers. He does not speak merely to a circle of the initiated. Despite his learning, he wrote in such a fashion that any intelligent person interested in his subject can read him. He is a master of language and of suasion; he creates an unbroken series of forceful images; he uses words in unusual ways to achieve certain effects; and, most important, he can create a self-sufficient reality within the covers of a book. One can read Grønbech as one might great poetry—in order to partake of an emotional experience, to discover a thesaurus of imagery and striking descriptions, and to feel the force of rhythm

13

and rhetorical devices. That is to say, the poetic nature of his writing and the power of his language can be sensed in almost any of his works, as different as those works may be substantively one from the other. In order to ascertain Grønbech's impelling qualities as a writer, it is not necessary to read his novels and poetry; in fact, these works do not represent him at his most impressive, either as a creator of metaphysical realities or as a linguistic wizard.

It is quite justifiable to speak of Vilhelm Grønbech as a great writer, but he cannot be characterized under the usual rubrics of lyrics, drama, and prose narrative. Thousands of his countrymen read him and heard him lecture, and many were carried away in part by his command of the language, by the strength of his convictions, and by the striking quality of his metaphors and other rhetorical figures when he dealt with philosophical, religious, and literary subjects. While Grønbech did publish several volumes of poetry and two novels, his significance is not as a contributor to Danish imaginative literature. He is, nevertheless, noteworthy in the history of that literature, as can be demonstrated from the many allusions to him by imaginative writers in the 1940s and 1950s and, in particular, through the role that he played for the persons associated with the periodical *Heretica*, which was published between 1948 and 1953 and served as a gathering point for a number of influential post–World War II intellectuals. This particular facet of Grønbech has faded into the background since the demise of *Heretica;* and an awareness of Grønbech is not peculiarly associated with any particular group or movement in Danish literature. This is as it should be, for Grønbech was never a partisan or sectarian thinker; indeed, it is not possible to circumscribe accurately what his own religious—not to mention political—convictions must have been.

Characteristic for Grønbech is his astonishing ability to identify himself with a chosen subject and to write about that subject as if he accepted its theses and principles. In this way he makes various figures from the past come alive and seem real, and he conveys to the reader a congenial response toward whatever person, culture, or phenomenon he is depicting. Grønbech is nevertheless able at the same time to express himself in a new, independent, and memorable fashion and in such a way that he is difficult to refute, even though the reader may be convinced that Grønbech himself did not share the convictions and beliefs about which he wrote so incisively and so apparently sympathetically. Grønbech's style might superficially be characterized as dynamic or even mesmeric, to judge by the effect that his words, both spoken and written, had upon many of his hearers and readers in the 1930s and 1940s. Even three decades after his death, Grønbech's work exudes an unusual aura and captivates readers by virtue of his striking generalities and authoritative syntheses. Since his death it has become easier to be critical toward him; he brooked no contradiction during his lifetime. Now, however, it is possible to read him more objectively and to weigh his opinions against the opinions of other historians of culture and religion.

Grønbech was not agitating for any particular religion. Through his philological and historical studies he came to realize that religion—or the lack thereof—was ultimately the greatest single force in the development of man. As a consequence, the forms of expression and practice that organized religion has assumed in the past were viewed as worthy of analysis, depiction, and explanation. Likewise, religious leaders of the past had a claim to attention as men and women who, as much as kings or dictators or generals— and many times more profoundly than such wielders of temporal power—have had an impact on society and determined the course of history. For Vilhelm Grønbech, the depiction of a religion was not a pragmatic and historical exercise focusing upon outward and objective phenomena. The superficial history of a religious movement is relatively easy to determine; the actual basis of belief and the driving forces either within an organized religion or acting upon an important religious figure are often a different matter. Efforts have been made to interpret religious movements on a psychological basis or on a social basis. Such efforts, while simplifications, should not be discounted entirely, but they do not produce any wholly satisfactory explanation of the phenomena of religion. Grønbech, like various other historians of religion, was a psychologist or a sociologist only insofar as he needed insight into the disciplines of psychology and sociology in order to achieve his goal of a more penetrating interpretive presentation.

The historian of religion is concerned with the basic forces of human existence and cannot be expected to produce explanations that are satisfactory and at the same time simple, uniform, and universally applicable. The sympathetic understanding of religious phenomena from various parts of the world and from various eras requires a kind of tolerance that few persons possess. Most human beings are wedded to their parochial and inherited religious and philosophical beliefs; and while they may tolerate the beliefs of others, they find it difficult to be so tolerant as to be actually able to admit that some other philosophical and religious system can have, indeed does have, the same validity as the one to which they subscribe. Grønbech is remarkable because he did possess this tolerance, and to such a degree that he seems to have posited multiple systems of belief as actually coexistent if not mutually compatible. Fundamental to Grønbech's method and approach is this acceptance of multiple reality. While most readers will probably admit that what they in their own time accept as real may not necessarily be looked upon as real sometime in the future, Grønbech was willing to admit that there were concurrent realities and that each had its claim to acceptability. All of these realities were, to be sure, based upon a physical actuality—of air and soil, heat and light, let us say—that he did not dispute. The several realities were, however, wholly acceptable to him. Not only might he describe the reality of some metaphysical system with understanding, but he could subscribe to the thesis that the one reality was as indisputable as the other. In a way, this attitude regarding the coexistence of several realities must be considered helpful to a historian of religion who would not judge religions (other than his own) purely from a confessional viewpoint. Grønbech was able to identify himself with other religious, philosophical, and metaphysical systems and apparently accept them wholeheartedly in order to depict and explain them to his readers. This was not a pose, but a consequence of the espousal of the aforementioned unusual principle: the concept of multiple reality.

He did not proceed on the assumption that there is but one truth or that we of the twentieth century possess the truth or are indeed heading nearer to it than those of any previous century. For Grønbech, truth is absolutely relative and therefore exists in any serious metaphysical system in which men sincerely and naively believe. Our century, he lets us know, is insecure for the very reason that it is so detached and objective. Here Grønbech is a good representative of our own times. He can admit truth in the past but not in the present, since he accepts a metaphysical relativity in his catholicity.

In Grønbech's opinion, nevertheless, all systems of religious belief did have a common denominator, namely, the fact that each system is built upon some set of basic assumptions. These basic assumptions are, however, not necessarily readily distinguishable *per se*. It was Grønbech's contention that they had in each case to be deduced by linguistic means, that is, by a penetration to what the linguist today might call the deep structure of language from which all working concepts and religious vocabulary can be derived.

Grønbech did not make an observation to this effect in any programmatic way, but proceeded *in medias res*. In his first great work, *Vor folkeæt i oldtiden (The Culture of the Teutons)*, he attempted to identify such concepts—which could be equated with certain words—without which the entire structure of religion and the life of the Germanic peoples would be inexplicable. In so doing, Grønbech, who had not been trained as a historian of religion, was applying his philological knowledge in a radical and fruitful way.

The foundation for *The Culture of the Teutons* was philological in that the study concerned itself above all with the denotations and connotations of certain key terms in the culture of the pre-Christian Germanic past. Grønbech's penetrating examination of these terms led him to a consideration of the basic beliefs of any people or peoples who used them—and the basic beliefs of any people quite simply constitute their religion. This method of investigation turned out to be profitable and stimulating. It was apparently also a method that could be employed elsewhere with comparable results. Moreover, since those results dealt with the basic assumptions of human existence, they were a worthy subject for further consideration by a thinking man.

To be sure, Grønbech had not invented a cut and dried method that could be applied mechanically to one phenomenon after the other. The basic linguistic approach of the historian of religion was, however, as applicable in a consideration of Hellenistic culture of classical antiquity as it was in an analysis of Germanic culture of the Middle Ages.

Because his concern is with the essence of his subjects, Grønbech's observations do not become outdated. He discerns the ultimate concepts of writers and thinkers, of ritual and belief, and portrays their essential qualities. His conclusions are based on a familiarity with source material—not merely details or single aspects of the material but a synthetic whole, which he would describe. His is often a fresh and individual—and subjective—approach. If his interpretation cannot be accepted, that is not a consequence of the progression of scholarly investigation and the revelation of new truth, but because Grønbech's own subjectivity is unacceptable. His recasting of the material is often identifiable as the work of a creative mind, of an imaginative scholar, rather than of a writer who is primarily a critic or an historian. His interpretation has its own intrinsic validity, and can be rejected as an interpretation without losing all philosophical value. At the same time that Grønbech is interpreting and analysing, he is intimating his own philosophy, which, after an examination of his many synthetic works from first to last, does not turn out necessarily to be unified.

Grønbech's concern was ever the basic assumptions of human existence as they are found in established metaphysical systems, notably in various religions but also in social patterns of certain societies in the past and present, and in those figures whose words or whose works have made a crucial difference in the development of Western man: Jesus, Goethe, William Blake, Friedrich Schlegel, Saint Paul, Saint Theresa, Wordsworth, and Herder, among others. Grønbech wrote essays or books about all these figures, in order to reinterpret them as well as to plumb their thoughts and to delineate those concepts that were of central importance to them. He was constantly involved in reinterpretation, and not only in reassessment, but also in revaluation.

While Grønbech lectured on the history of religion in the University of Copenhagen for three decades, we should not be surprised that, despite the breadth and encompassing nature of his work, there were numerous subjects and persons to whom he might have addressed his attention, but did not. Thus, for example, Grønbech does not discuss Martin Luther, although he is writing as a Lutheran in a Lutheran country. Nor does he grapple with the Reformation as a phenomenon.

Grønbech speaks about the past and interprets the thoughts of the past as something living and believable. He does not judge from a standpoint of superiority. He makes it possible for a reader to understand the plausibility of an older *Weltanschauung*. Grønbech writes with such conviction that one is inclined to believe that he is expressing his own beliefs and that he accepts the *Weltanschauung* that he momentarily is attempting to interpret.

Vilhelm Grønbech's method may be called intuitive. He thoroughly familiarized himself with the written sources and then interpreted them, convinced that his readings and interpretation were not mere possibilities or hypothesis but were correct. With

Grønbech there was no argument. He spoke authoritatively, if not always with absolute clarity. What he said was often a reformulation. He believed that he understood the heart of a matter about which he expressed himself. He was not concerned with detailed scholarly documentation, however, and his writings do not lend themselves to easily perceptible documentation, since he rarely quoted directly or cited specific instances. Rather, he employed the general paraphrase or the interpretive paraphrase, and relied strongly upon metaphor.

Men turn to the most incisive critics for an understanding and reinterpretation of the events of the past, of the intellectual achievements of the past, of the literary monuments of the past, and of the great minds of the past. Grønbech is such a critic. He tends to focus his attention on figures that cannot be dismissed from cultural history—from Saint Paul to Darwin, from Buddha to Goethe—and to provide insight and comprehension that we have not possessed before. He was never one to speak in a querulous voice; he expresses himself with conviction about his own analyses—analyses that were generated slowly, after he had assimilated the evidence at hand and turned matters over and over in his mind until he could produce a satisfactory synthesis.

The figures and subjects to which he addressed himself do not represent an arbitrary or eclectic selection. His *œuvre* possesses an organic quality when judged from the standpoint of philosophical rationale or subject matter. It is characteristic of Grønbech that the nuclei of later works are to be found in earlier works, as one readily observes when one looks upon his production in retrospect. Thus, as early as 1922, he wrote entire chapters about Herder, Schlegel, and Goethe—authors about whom he would later publish books—in *Religiøse strømninger i det nittende aarhundrede (Religious Currents in the Nineteenth Century)*. There is, incidentally, a curious sort of arithmetic progression in Grønbech's production. The bulk of it is concentrated in the last fifteen years of his life. After *The Culture of the Teutons* was completed in 1912, he published only a few shorter works and some essays until 1922, when *Religious Currents* appeared. Three years later the first volume of the series of books on mystics *(Mystikere i Europa og Indien)* was published— but the next two volumes did not appear until 1932, when Grønbech was nearly sixty. After that, however, the publication in book form multiplied: One good-sized volume each in 1933 and 1934, three in

1935, one in 1939, five in 1940, two each in 1941 and 1942, and a half dozen more before Grønbech began a surprisingly large production of essays in a periodical he edited between 1946 and 1948.

Grønbech not only grew more prolific but acquired a new status in the 1930s and 1940s, years of depression and great political unrest in Denmark as elsewhere in Europe, for he, more profoundly than most, could both sense and identify the needs of his fellow men; and, he had the strength to face what seemed to be chaos and nevertheless to seek and to recognize patterns of existence. Above all, he articulated what he felt to be the greatest need of his contemporaries, a need for myth—or one might say in more pedestrian terms, a need for something to believe in. This is a recurrent theme in Grønbech's work, a leitmotif in his addresses and his analyses of religions and of literature. Harmony was for him the first goal of existence, but it could be achieved only when man possessed myth, and when man believed not as an individual but as a member of a society of believers—that is, only when the individual was a part of a community.

Despite Grønbech's repeated cry for a community of believers, he could not be said himself to have belonged to any extant embryonic or incipient community of believers. He stood always as a man alone and as an original thinker. Like Goethe or any other great figure in the history of culture, Grønbech drew upon many resources. He was well read, he synthesized his ideas from a multitude of other writers, but one cannot put one's finger on this work or that, this writer or that writer who was of singular importance for Grønbech—unless it be his teacher of philology at the University of Copenhagen, Vilhelm Thomsen, from whom Grønbech had learned the philological-linguistic method that he employed in much of his research and to whom Grønbech dedicated *The Culture of the Teutons* in both the original Danish and the English editions.

What Grønbech did not do was to provide his fellow men with a religion. He pointed out the need to believe and he pointed out the need for myth; but he did not describe the myth or offer a myth that one should accept and believe in. He has often been called a prophet by Danes, but the identification is inaccurate; he was not a prophet but an analyst and a synthesist, a critic and a historian. He would help his fellow men see more clearly, in order both to understand the past and to understand the significance of a metaphysical existence and the importance of a metaphysical system, although he was aware that any such system is man-made. The care and apparent sympathy with which he described a system or any religious figure might lead one to assume that Grønbech had found a myth that should be accepted by our time, but no such myth was consonant with Grønbech's overall utterances. Even though he might accept the existence of a myth's reality and validity at some time in the past or for some society other than his own, he was never engaged in proselytization.

Although not politically active, Grønbech became something of a demagogue in the years of the German occupation, for his audiences suddenly multiplied and he, who was used to speaking to a small group of students at the university, was addressing an auditorium full of interested listeners at a teachers' college in Copenhagen. Beginning about the time of World War I, he had given many public addresses, most of which were reported in the press, and in these he proved to be incisive and provocative. A broader appeal to a larger public came toward the end of his life, however, and after World War II this continued for a short time through the publication of a periodical that he and Hal Koch, professor of ecclesiastical history in the University of Copenhagen, edited and to which Grønbech was the major contributor during the three years prior to his death in 1948. This periodical, entitled *Frie Ord—Free Words*—enjoyed an unexpectedly large circulation. In it Grønbech was able to speak out as a critic of the times—his first essay in the periodical was on the atom bomb—but at the same time to agitate for those ideas that had informed all of his works since the publication of the first volume of *The Culture of the Teutons* in 1909.

Grønbech was an impelling and impressive speaker. He often lectured without notes, but his thoughts were clearly organized and compelling. It was next to impossible not to believe what he said when he said it. He was never at a loss for words or for the right words. He was not given to discussion, however, and did not suffer fools gladly. His authoritative manner might be considered arrogant and offensive today, but in the years of his tenure as professor at the University of Copenhagen, his listeners accorded him considerabe reverence. It would have been a rare individual who possessed the quickness of wit, a sufficiently large vocabulary, an adequate command of metaphor, and the broad knowledge of facts that would enable him to question, not to mention refute, anything that Grønbech said.

In the English-speaking world Vilhelm Grønbech has remained little known. His *Culture of the Teutons*, a revised translation into

English of *Vor Folkeæt i Oldtiden,* appeared in 1931 but did not reach a wide audience. The work, upon which his international fame rests, has appeared in several editions in German. Grønbech received considerable recognition for this four-volume study when it was first published (1909–1912); because of it, he received a call—which he did not accept—to the University of Leipzig. More recently, numerous other works by Grønbech have appeared in German translation; some works have appeared in Swedish; and individual translations have been made into Dutch and Finnish. An English translation of his examination of the major philosophical currents of the nineteenth century was issued in 1964, and republished in the centenary of Grønbech's birth in 1973, but the vast body of work remains unavailable in English—items most of which have been published in more than one edition and have appealed to various groups of Danish readers, upon most of whom Grønbech has made a lasting impression. While there are parallels that may be drawn between Grønbech and two other better-known Danish writers—Søren Kierkegaard and Georg Brandes—such parallels are misleading to the point of inviting invidious comparison. Ironically enough, Vilhelm Grønbech had an antagonistic attitude to both his countrymen. He disagreed basically with Kierkegaard's religious conviction of the primary necessity of the salvation of the individual. He was skeptical of Brandes' originality and treatment of sources and wrote in a very different fashion from Brandes although, curiously enough, on several of the same topics to which Brandes had addressed himself.

Grønbech's impact upon many of his readers has been so profound and pervasive that it is time to assess his position on the Scandinavian cultural scene and to provide readers of English a general introduction to his *œuvre.* His collected works comprise some forty volumes. They deal with many subjects, but essentially with interrelated philosophical and religious questions pertaining to the basic assumptions behind human existence as interpreted through the examples furnished by various cultures of the past and by various thinkers and poets. While it is easy to point out Grønbech's major areas of interest—the culture of Germanic antiquity, of Hellenistic Rome, of classical antiquity, and of early Christianity, to each of which Grønbech devoted multivolume studies—some of his most effective formulations are found in the shorter works and in numerous of his essays which treat more specific, limited topics.

CHAPTER 2

Assessing Germanic Antiquity

I Basic Metaphysical Concepts

W HEN the first volume of his study of early Germanic culture appeared in 1909, Grønbech was lecturer in English literature at the University of Copenhagen. The three-volume sequel, which appeared in 1912 and completed the work that in Danish is entitled *Vor Folkeæt i Oldtiden* (literally "Our Race in Olden Times" but was translated into English in 1931 as *The Culture of the Teutons*), projected Grønbech's name onto the academic firmament and endowed him with a position in the history of culture and of religion that he was to maintain until his death in 1948. By then he had been professor of the history of religion at the University of Copenhagen for over thirty years. In 1909, the book must have taken even his colleagues somewhat by surprise, for Grønbech had begun his academic career as a student of language under the aegis of a distinguished older philologist, Vilhelm Thomsen. His dissertation had dealt with Turkish phonology, and the second scholarly publication to appear under his name was a vocabulary of the dialect of Bokhara, in 1905. In the interim he had, to be sure, published a slight volume of poetry entitled *Morituri*, but it had been issued anonymously and was not widely distributed. As if these credentials were not in themselves incongruous enough, Grønbech had, since acquiring his doctorate in 1902, been organist in a church in Copenhagen and had for a time also been employed in the Royal Library. That he had been appointed lecturer in English at the University of Copenhagen was testimony not of his familiarity with English literature, but rather of his brilliance, promise, and broad interests, which older professors at the university had recognized. In order to obtain his services for the University of Copenhagen, the university administration had appointed Grønbech to a lectureship

23

that seemed to have little bearing either on what he had done previously or on the research work with which he currently was engaged. The lectureship was no sinecure, however, and Grønbech was actively engaged in lecturing on various English authors while he held it. Subsequently he published an essay on Wordsworth and another on Donne, and discussed several English writers in a work central to his production: the volume which in English is entitled *Religious Currents of the Nineteenth Century (Religiøse strømninger i det nittende aarhundrede,* 1922). Moreover, he wrote a monograph on William Blake that appeared in 1933.

The publication of the first volume of *The Culture of the Teutons* immediately attracted considerable attention to Grønbech and resulted in his being offered a professorship at the University of Leipzig. Once again the authorities at the University of Copenhagen had to act in order to keep Grønbech in Denmark, and as a consequence created for him an extraordinary professorship in the history of religion. From now on Grønbech is in the first instance a historian of religion, albeit not religion conceived in any sectarian or narrow sense. That is, he did not function as an ecclesiastical historian; he was, rather, a researcher into those metaphysical concepts that are basic to any system of belief and that therefore are the mainstays of a culture.

The appearance of Grønbech's work in 1909 meant a new departure in the history of religion and understandably caused consternation in some quarters. There were those who felt that Grønbech was taking too many liberties with the texts and those who believed that he was something of a fantast. Grønbech was also criticized for not having made sufficient use of classical sources, notably Tacitus and Caesar; but all these charges in fact helped delineate the peculiarities and the virtues of Grønbech's innovative interpretation. On the one hand, one could criticize Grønbech for being a poor historian, while on the other, one could excuse him as not being a historian at all. He was an interpreter of the past, with emphasis on the history of religion. His was a subjective interpretation despite his familiarity with sources. If his words did not constitute the whole truth as others know it, they nevertheless served to awaken, to inspire, and to arouse.

The first volume of *The Culture of the Teutons* is entitled in Danish *Lykkemand og Niding,* that is, it embraces the extremes of metaphysical existence in Old Icelandic literature: the terms identify the man who enjoys luck and the man who does not. The contrast is not so sharply made in the English version of the book, where the title of volume I has disappeared; there is no English equivalent for the word *lykkemand* (although the term *niding*, while unusual, is used in English).

One can explain what Grønbech was doing in *The Culture of the Teutons* in relatively few words, but it is impossible to convey an idea of the content of the work without a dependence on Grønbech's terminology and without at least using the chapter headings that he employs. In fact, in attempting to describe Grønbech's works, the critic is constantly tempted to quote Grønbech, not merely because of the forcefulness of his diction and imagery, but because of the substance of his presentation and argument. This is a notable characteristic—and weakness—of the two book length studies of Grønbech that have appeared in Danish within the last few years. The critic wants to encourage his reader to familiarize himself with Grønbech firsthand and feels, understandably, that Grønbech can best formulate his own ideas. This means shifting a considerable burden of proof upon the reader; and since Grønbech himself used quotations extensively, there is also frequently a danger of second-hand quotations that can serve no avowed purpose of interpretation.

In volume I of *The Culture of the Teutons,* Grønbech addresses himself to several concepts—*frith*, honor, luck, and the *niding;* to several relationships—honor in the clan, luck in the clan, life and soul, the soul and the clan, and the structure of the clan; and to the two unique and inevitable events of birth and death. All these words and concepts are explicated by references to a long series of events and situations drawn from older Germanic literature, and by not simply using them as examples, but rather as visible expressions of underlying and unspoken assumptions of the culture of which they are a part. The abundance of evidence that Grønbech provides on each point in his discussion is sufficient to convince the reader of the validity of his conclusions regarding the existence of a substratum of philosophically and psychologically determining factors that were so pervasive in Germanic culture that they scarcely required elucidation. And yet without a categorization of many acts and events, the unity of thought that informed that culture is not immediately perceived. By very close reading, particularly of Icelandic sagas, and by reflection upon many parallel situations or parallel outward actions, Grønbech was able to penetrate into the world of the unspoken

assumptions of Germanic antiquity and to identify and label the
essential qualities that could be deduced through a comparative
analysis of much seemingly disparate human action which is reported in some detail in the Icelandic sagas and recorded less fully
in other Germanic monuments.

Grønbech stresses the inviolability and absoluteness of those
basic qualities which he was able to deduce from the preserved
written evidence. He has made himself familiar with all available
source material, and with such thoroughness and intimacy that he is
able to assume with relative assurance that he knows why persons in
Germanic antiquity had to act the way they did.

In *The Culture of the Teutons*, then, single concepts have been
subjected to detailed analysis and description. They are seen to
represent the summing up of a very large amount of analytical
examination and thought on Grønbech's part in an attempt to distill
into crucial terms thes essence of pre-Christian Germanic culture.
The word that is the subject of chapter I may appear somewhat
problematical both in Danish and in English: *frith*. Grønbech chose
to employ the term *frith*, a loan word from Icelandic in both Danish
and English, presumably for two reasons: first, because it embodied
a concept that he recognized as fundamental and central in Germanic antiquity, and second, because the term was not burdened
with connotations for the Danish or English reader. It is almost
frivolous to attempt a definition of *frith* in a few sentences when
Grønbech has used a chapter of some forty pages to describe what
the concept denotes and connotes. Suffice it to say here, however,
that *frith*, which is etymologically the same as the word for peace in
some of the Germanic languages (German *Friede,* Danish *fred)*, is
identified as a broad concept of the relation of men to one another,
depending on the kind of relationship that is given between individuals, kinsmen, or friends. In volume I of *The Culture of the
Teutons*, Grønbech comes close to a summary definition that may
help us understand the concept *frith*. He speaks of it as "a love
which can only be characterised as a feeling of identity, so deeply
rooted that neither sympathy nor antipathy, nor any humour or
mood can make it ebb or flow. No happening can be so powerful as
to reach down and disturb this depth."[1] The phrase "this depth" is
noteworthy, for it suggests that Grønbech is plumbing a metaphysical world and seeking those assumptions of existence that are so
nearly fundamental that they are either taken for granted or over-

looked. The originality of Grønbech's interpretation is indicative of his preeminent position in the history of culture and religion.

In addition to *frith*, the major concepts that Grønbech perceives as informing Old Icelandic literature, and presumably therefore Germanic antiquity, are honor and luck. After a detailed investigation of these concepts as they are found in his sources, Grønbech goes on to describe man in early Scandinavian society and the most important functions that life had in that society. Indeed, one chapter is entitled "The Art of Life." Grønbech discusses the ideas of birth, death, and immortality; the structure of the clan; and the importance of genealogy. He describes also the unfortunate person who is himself without luck and who, within the context of the Old Germanic culture, is unreliable and therefore demonic. This sort of person is called the *niding*.

Grønbech goes on to identify what were considered treasures in the Germanic past, as well as the role of the gift, the significance of names, the implications of eating and drinking in common, the formalistic practice of religion, the nature of the sacrifice and the festival, and finally, the evidence of Old Norse–Icelandic mythology in ritual as well as in daily activities.

Here, as in numerous other places in several of his books, Grønbech stresses the importance of the ritual and, as he puts it, the creative festival. It was by means of the festival, where men gathered, believed, and worked together, that a certain harmony was achieved, a feeling of kinship and community: A sense of belonging was impressed upon the minds of the participants. The ceremonial act gave body and reality to the myth. In one sense, writes Grønbech, "It may be said with some truth that man creates his gods in the festival."[2] "The character of the feast," he continues, "lies in the fact that individual men are completely set aside or disappear, and their place is taken up for the time by that which is supreme everfelt reality: the clan or its hamingja *W*an Icelandic word for luck*E*, its past and present and future ages in one." Later in volume II he expressed himself more forcibly and succinctly: "The ritual moves in a region of speech above the commonplace dialogue of every day; it gives birth to a vocabulary abounding in metaphors and images. . . . [T]his his formal speech is poetry, because it is the passionate language of life at its highest and strongest moments. . . ."[3]

What we call poetry and myth is ultimately nothing but history,

Grønbech avers, but to read about the meaning of tradition as it was handed down in the festival is not enough to enable one to understand the words spoken or sung; one must be able to hear as well as to see.

Understandably, it was the first volume of Grønbech's *Culture of the Teutons* that attracted the most attention and the most criticism when it appeared in 1909. The convictions and principles that guided Grønbech while completing the work remained the same, although the aspects of antique Germanic culture with which he was concerned shifted and his attention became more concentrated on single facets of his subject. That some of the early critics were not aware of Grønbech's intent and charged him with being an unsatisfactory historian because he did not draw on such time-honored sources as Tacitus is understandable—but Grønbech was, of course, not attempting to write traditional history, but to explain culture and religion. As an interpreter of the past he had few direct antecedents, although Grønbech's teacher Valdemar Vedel had published a work on heroic poetry in 1903 that may be looked upon as a forerunner for Grønbech's study, in part because it attempted to create a synthesis, in part because it was broad in its interpretation, and in part because it was neither historical or sociological in its conception. Otherwise one can note only that Grønbech was familiar with and drew upon a vast number of secondary works pertaining to Germanic antiquity, although his utilization of such secondary material remained less significant and less apparent than his own treatment of primary sources. Grønbech knew the classical sources that he did not cite, as is clearly demonstrated in the first volume of his study, in which he explains why he believes that the Latin writers who mention the Germanic peoples were not transmitting a historically reliable image.

There were also those early critics who pointed out that much of what Grønbech said about Germanic antiquity also had validity in other earlier cultures. While this criticism perhaps was not necessarily meant to be positive, it was in truth a recognition of one of Grønbech's goals: He wanted to ascertain those characteristics common to cultures and religions that hitherto had been labeled with the pejorative and misleading term "primitive." He was, moreover, interested in calling attention to any culture that could be identified as having a religion of harmony. One might say that

Grønbech was attempting to recognize and define the essence of religion, which is the key that permits one to deduce the nature of all other elements of existence for a group of believers. Earlier critics also overlooked the fact that Grønbech always wrote with an eye to the present. Time and again parallels may be drawn between Germanic antiquity and contemporary society. And scattered throughout his study, particularly in the notes, are observations that are socially critical and transcend time. Culture, Grønbech was to write in the introduction to the English version, *The Culture of the Teutons,* "means an elastic harmony between man's inner self and his surroundings, so that he is able not only to make his environment serve his material ends, but also to transfigure the impulses of the surrounding world into spiritual ideals and aspirations."[4]

II *A View of the World*

In the second volume of *The Culture of the Teutons,* which bears the Danish title *Midgård og Menneskelivet (Middle Realm*—that is, the earth—*and Human Life),* Grønbech tries to make his reader comprehend how the Germanic peoples viewed the world about them and what their attitudes were toward the most common events of life and to relations among individuals. The principal sources upon which he drew were the Old English *Beowulf* and Old Icelandic sagas. Central to his argument was an examination of certain aspects of vocabulary. In particular he pointed to the great specificity in Old English and Old Icelandic as indicated by the vast number of synonyms for certain terms in those languages. The multitude of words for "sea" for example, could not, Grønbech warned, be explained simply as a use for poetic alternatives and variation. The activities and needs of a people who lived by and from the sea necessarily gave rise to a maritime vocabulary of many particular denotative terms that now are lost because modern man has become more casual in his relationship to the sea and less dependent on its whims. In Germanic antiquity, however, precision of expression in certain areas of endeavor and experience was important and could be achieved only by a highly specialized vocabulary. This wealth of synonyms did not mean that the Germanic peoples were incapable of abstractions, however.

The contrast between life and nonlife would, superficially, seem

self-evident and simple. Grønbech's probing analysis of his source
material makes it clear to the reader, however, that our concept of
life today is not identical with the concept of life at various times in
the past. A brief reflection on the question of how far the soul can be
separated from the body either metaphysically or in the physical
world is sufficient to suggest the complexity and the implications of
the problem that Grønbech was discussing. Grønbech believes that
many of the metaphors that employ terms taken from nature had
their origins in a conviction that some part of nature that we would
consider either not alive or capable only of personification was indeed alive in a sense that we would not admit today. The attempt to
define the boundaries of the concept of life in Germanic antiquity
leads quickly to an attempt to define the soul. It is not surprising
that Grønbech is confronted with almost insurmountable difficulties at this juncture. Although he cannot be said to have produced a
satisfactory definition that either includes all the elements that constitute the soul or excludes all the elements that do not constitute
the soul, he is able to recognize certain characteristics that were
essential to the soul for the Germanic peoples. In the first instance
these essential elements embrace the ideas of honor and good fortune that he had discussed in the first volume of *The Culture of the
Teutons*. To these ideas he adds other concepts from Old Norse:
concepts of force, of courage, and of life.

Grønbech also discusses the concept of kinship at length in the
second volume. He makes a particular point of the significance of
genealogies as they are found in Old Icelandic literature. The tendency in modern times has always been at best to read through the
genealogies quickly and pay them no mind. Grønbech makes the
simple observation that since the genealogies are regularly present,
they must be assumed to have a significant function. In his opinion
they contribute to the extension of the life of the individuals mentioned and grant a kind of immortality. Moreover, they suggest the
importance of names and of the transfer of names from one person to
another. As in so many places in *The Culture of the Teutons*, Grønbech's observations here have validity for the present. The reader
understands perhaps for the first time that naming children has a
metaphysical motivation; there is often the unexpressed wish that
the namesake will somehow inherit the characteristics of the person
for whom he is named. In other words, one senses an underlying
belief in metempsychosis.

Finally, Grønbech reminds us that the nature of kinship is not necessarily as simple as it might seem at first glance and that the concept of who was a kin to someone else in Germanic antiquity was not identical with the degrees of kinship in more recent times.

III *Supernatural Forces*

The third volume of *The Culture of the Teutons* was originally entitled *Hellighed og Helligdom (Sanctity and Sanctuary)*. Through the use of a large number of examples, it attempts to make comprehensible how objects were informed with a supernatural force. This force was most frequently felt to bestow good fortune on him who possessed a certain object or who received it as a gift. In this connection Grønbech stresses the importance of gifts exchanged between friends—such gifts were not merely incidental to friendship but were in fact a corollary of it. Once more the reader sees simple parallels from his own experience. Objects formerly owned by certain people are particularly attractive or repulsive to him. That is, the objects themselves are felt to possess some force that has been absorbed from their previous owners. We in the twentieth century would attempt to explain away this phenomenon merely as psychological association; it is nevertheless real and provides insight into an earlier time that was not blessed with our sophisticated psychological explanations. While Grønbech admits the existence of symbolism, he stresses that the function of the gift or the belief in luck identified by the certain object is not merely symbolic. Not only movable objects but also places in the natural world were and are thought to be sources of supernatural power or good fortune. Other sacred places were created by the hand of man; but, curiously enough, we have next to no knowledge about the temples of Germanic antiquity, so it is not possible to speak more than fleetingly of the function of the temple or what was in the temple or to define the attitude of an ancient Scandinavian when he observed some event taking place in the temple.

Eating and drinking with others also had a sacred function, and Grønbech points out that drinking in particular was combined with a belief about the supernatural force connected with certain beverages at a time when there was no knowledge of the chemistry of alcohol. Then, as now, a person's character was observed sometimes to be affected by what he drank.

IV   Gods and Men

The fourth and final volume of Grønbech's study of the culture of
Germanic antiquities is entitled in Danish *Menneskelivet og
Guderne (Human Life and the Gods)*. The volume's brevity reminds
us how limited is our knowledge of the practice of religion in the
Germanic past. Grønbech attempts to account for the attitude of
Germanic man toward his gods; the interaction of men and gods,
and the cultivation of the gods through worship, ceremony, sacrifice, prayer, and celebration. This volume is at the same time the
most factual and the most speculative in the series: Grønbech pays
more attention to providing the reader with historical data taken
from his sources than in the other volumes, but because of the
paucity of information regarding the indigenous religion of the
Germanic peoples, he is frequently driven to hypothesis in order to
create more than a fragmentary picture. Always the philologist, he
seeks those words that can serve as keys to open the closed doors of
a forgotten religion. As a cultural historian he is also conscious of
those remnants of a superseded culture that have lived on into the
present. The most easily discernible in Scandinavia is the custom of
drinking a *skaal*, for there is a marked element of ritual still in such
drinking in the Northern countries. In Scandinavia as elsewhere,
many of the annual festivals of today contain suggestions of their
non-Christian origin. Their earlier significance is no longer understood, but tradition preserves certain actions and certain symbols
that enjoy an aura of religious respectability.

Grønbech's view of the religion and mythology of Germanic antiquity was in contradistinction to dominant accepted hypotheses at
the beginning of the twentieth century, when it was still in vogue to
attempt to explain mythology as a kind of nature symbolism or
simply as the misinterpretation of natural phenomena. Here and
elsewhere Grønbech realized that so-called primitive man was far
from primitive in the sense of being simple. He understood that
primitive religion was complex religion, and he brought to it broad
sympathy and understanding. Grønbech's method is to no small
extent derived from the linguistic studies that preceded his concern
with mythology and religion. He had gone through an exacting
schooling in philology as a disciple of Vilhelm Thomsen and was
applying some of the techniques of linguistics, notably a scien-
tifically exacting concern with the meaning and derivation of an

individual word, to those terms that formed the nucleus of a mythology. This impression is reinforced by a number of etymologies, which comprise the series of "additional notes" appended to the English-language version of *The Culture of the Teutons*. For Grønbech, every designatory word was rooted in the experience of the people who used that word; the word drew its force "from the harmony of experience that makes up reality."[5] The historian, he was to observe later in his book *Sprogets Musik (The Music of Language*, 1943), has to exert himself to acquire a language word for word: "When he has learned what God, soul, life, or death are called by people of the past, then begins the attempt to trace the meanings of these words, their extent, breadth, depth, tone, and force."[6] Grønbech continued by stating that psychological and spiritual truth is more important than literal translation or mere historical fact. Such truth, he felt, could be achieved only by the most penetrating examination of concepts, and concepts represented by words in the documentary evidence. "The only way the scholar can gain an understanding of the past," he was to write in 1941 in his book *Kristus*, "is to become a confidant of the people of the time in question; soberly and patiently he must read the documents which have been handed down and attempt to understand their meaning in order to achieve that which establishes the directions of those peoples' thoughts and the fruits of their fantasy. In this way he will discover what was real to them."[7] We speak of our critical method, he observed, as a means to extract the kernel of truth, but our work often consists in peeling off the husk and throwing away the fruit. Our historical investigation is an attempt to translate one reality into the terms of a different one, and there is a danger that truth evaporates during the process. He was conscious of the danger inherent in this method, however, and was to warn against it still later, in *Kampen for en ny sjæl (The Struggle for a new Soul*, 1946): "It is a false modernization of people of the past if one change their words according to one's own needs and get out of them what one seeks; this means that one is arranging their words in such a way that one gets to hear what one wishes to hear." Grønbech wished to achieve what he termed a more profound modernization, "when one penetrates to that which is central in man of the past and lets his experience expand within our own experience."[8]

The approach that Grønbech employed in *The Culture of the Teutons* is the same that he employed in his other major works.

First, he familiarized himself with all written evidence on the subject in hand. He then endeavored to ascertain what the underlying ideas were that informed the cultural phenomena with which he was dealing. He made an effort to isolate single concepts that might even be identifiable in single words that were essential to the culture, or one could say to the religious convictions upon which the culture was based. This is particularly striking in *The Culture of the Teutons* where Grønbech reduced his examination to relatively few words which he concluded were of primary significance in determining what was important in the literature of Scandinavian antiquity.

Athough *Vor Folkeæt i Oldtiden* bears the title *The Culture of the Teutons* in English and *Kultur und Religion der Germanen* in German translation, it is in fact an extrapolation primarily from Old Icelandic literature. How far the basic assumptions of Old Icelandic literature as identified and explained by Grønbech are identical with those of all early Germanic culture is debatable. The fact remains, however, that the only large amount of written evidence that we have about pre-Christian Germanic culture is preserved in Old Icelandic. It is therefore defensible to assume that some reasonable general conclusions regarding Germanic culture can be derived from the corpus of Old Icelandic literature, although to be sure that literature, while often heathen in spirit, was—insofar as we know it—recorded in Christian times, principally in the thirteenth and fourteenth centuries.

Just as we are uncertain about precisely when the Icelandic sagas were written down, so, too, we are uncertain about when the stories that they contain originated. Some of the time the sagas certainly tell of events that antedate Christianity, but there is a question as to how far back we may look and draw valid conclusions on the basis of written sources that date from the Christian era, even though the substance of a narrative antedates the introduction of Christianity. Grønbech nevertheless attempts to reconstruct the metaphysical world of Germanic antiquity through an analytical, interpretive, and intuitive process based primarily on the close reading of the Icelandic sagas.

That Grønbech did not make an effort to categorize the material with which he was working chronologically or geographically must be said to be a weakness of *The Culture of the Teutons*. He was, to be sure, endeavoring to determine the basic concepts of pre-Christian Germanic culture, presumably concepts that had had validity for a very long time. Nevertheless, it seems scarcely defensible to fail to identify from which century various bits of evidence come, in view of the extrinsic importance of certain striking historical events, such as the settlement of Iceland around the year 900 and the Christianization of the country just a century later. Grønbech ran the danger of inventing a metaphysical entity rather than recognizing and defining such an entity. Even though one grant the validity of all of his single hypotheses, the sum of the hypotheses could not correspond to a stated Germanic culture in any one place at a given time. It must be borne in mind, moreover, that the bulk of documentary evidence in which we can seek information about life in Germanic antiquity is derived from Icelandic manuscripts that date at the earliest from around the year 1200—or two centuries after the introduction of Christianity in Iceland. While some pre-Christian poetry, because of its form, may well have been preserved intact in that collection of lays known as the *Elder Edda,* one cannot assume that prose narratives in Old Icelandic faithfully reproduce the life or language of the pre-Christian era.

At this early date in Grønbech's career, it is already apparent that he is much concerned with the problem of harmony and that he is attracted to societies that have achieved a modicum of harmony. His introductory remarks are both typical and revealing. He is concerned with the existence of harmony, and he will attempt to identify himself with his subject even though this subject may be far removed from him both temporally and culturally. Because he perceived the existence of a harmony within Germanic society as represented by its literary monuments, he was drawn to it. His interest is therefore not merely antiquarian philological—unlike that of most scholars before him who had undertaken to examine and describe the same material.

Worth quoting here is the final paragraph of Grønbech's 1931 introduction to *The Culture of the Teutons:*

To appreciate the strength and the beauty of the culture of the ancient Teutons we must realise that their harmony is fundamentally unlike all that we possess or strive for, and consequently that all our immediate praising and blaming are futile. All things considered, we have little grounds for considering ourselves better judges than the classical onlookers. In our sentimental moments we lose ourselves in admiration of the heroism and splendid passion of our forefathers, but in our moments of historical analysis we pride ourselves on styling them barbarians, and this vacillation is in itself sufficient to show that in our appreciation we have not reached the centre whence the Teuton's thoughts and actions drew their life and strength. If we would enter into the minds of other peoples we must consent to discard our preconceived ideas as to what the world and man ought to be. It is not enough to admit a set of ideas as possible or even plausible: we must strive to reach a point of view from which these strange thoughts become natural; we must put off our own humanity as far as it is possible and put on another humanity for the time. We need, then, to begin quietly and modestly from the foundation, as knowing nothing at all, if we would understand what it was that held the soul of these men together, and made them personalities.[9]

V   *Variations on a Theme*

It is a curious fact that the revised and final version of Grønbech's *Vor Folkeæt i Oldtiden* is the English translation, *The Culture of the Teutons,* which was published in London and Copenhagen in 1931. By 1931 Grønbech's reputation had rested principally on this work for two decades, and it seemed desirable that the book be made available in a major language. The translation was undertaken by William Worster but with assistance from Grønbech himself, and a new section on the ritual drama was added. The English reworking thus became the revised canonical version of Grønbech's magnum opus. When, after Grønbech's death in 1948, a new Danish edition of the work was prepared, it was necessarily altered to correspond to the English edition. The English-speaking world is, therefore, fortunate to have a version of this work that the author himself helped produce and to which he gave an *imprimatur* in its translated form.

Subsequent to the completion of the Danish version of *The Culture of the Teutons* in 1912 Grønbech wrote four occasional essays that are more or less outgrowths of his magnum opus. The first of these, *Religionsskiftet i Norden (The Conversion of the North),* from the year 1913, is an extension of some of the arguments in *The Culture of the Teutons.* The second, *Primitiv religion* (first published in 1915), is a parallel study that contains a new interpretation of the concept "primitive." The third, the chapter devoted to old Scandinavian religion written for a composite history of religion edited by Edvard Lehmann in 1924, is simply a resumé of *The Culture of the Teutons.* The fourth essay, written in German for the fourth edition of Chantepie de la Saussaye's *Lehrbuch der Religionsgeschichte,* was also a summary of *The Culture of the Teutons* but with somewhat more emphasis on the historical elements of the subject and including a critical analysis of related works by other scholars.

In *The Conversion of the North* Grønbech makes the point that the Christianization of Iceland in the year 1000 cannot have been so sudden or unprepared or radical as the Icelandic sources would have us believe. He sees in the mass conversion a demonstration both of the closely knit quality of Old Icelandic society and of a peculiarly national religion that synthesized some elements from heathendom with Christianity when the new faith had been introduced into Scandinavia.

While Grønbech's view of primitive religion has been accepted by anthropologists and historians of religion today, it was a radical departure in the year 1915. Grønbech was a champion for a recognition of the complexities of so-called primitive culture, a culture that "possesses direct understanding of the nature around it." Grønbech points out that there is nothing simple about a so-called primitive religion and that it is quite as complicated as modern, sophisticated religion. He hesitates to designate any culture "primitive," and he points out that such a designation is in reality a revelation of our own astonishment that people can be different from us.[10] In his essay on Herder some years later, Grønbech was to say of primitive religions that they were "not a series of cunningly designed and elaborate dogmas and doctrines but the spontaneous representations of living folk belief which are born directly of experience."[11] At various places in his works one finds Grønbech returning to the question of "primitive" people and "primitive" religion. For example, in *Kristus* he points out that among the so-called primitive peoples individuals are not separated from one another by a bottomless chasm, nor is there a vacuum between man and nature: "While we stand outside and look at the surface of stones and trees and animals, they feel for every thing which lives and they seek to share feelings with it. Among such peoples, the souls of men are open, sensitive in a manner that we cannot even imagine."[12]

The thesis of Grønbech's early essay was epochal, and his arguments possess validity up to the present day, for misconceptions about so-called primitivism are still widespread. It is no accident that this essay from the year 1915 was reprinted in Johannes Pedersen's illustrated history of religion in 1948 and again in 1968; moreover, it was published separately as a paperback in 1963 and subsequently reprinted.

Incidentally, Grønbech's view of primitivism had as its corollary the rejection of missionary activity by Europeans among religious believers who possessed their own religious harmony. This was the point that Grønbech made in a lecture on "Primitive Religion" at an exhibition about missionary work held in Copenhagen in 1918. Grønbech took the position that representatives of various religions should endeavor to achieve mutual understanding and mutual respect, but not try to supplant the beliefs of one another. In this lecture he emphasized that the so-called primitive peoples are not undeveloped or half-developed, but that they are people of culture in the same sense of the word as we are.[13]

The résumé on old Scandinavian religion that was first published in 1924 and reprinted in 1948 (both times in the illustrated history of religion edited by Johannes Pedersen) can be useful to the reader who wants to familiarize himself quickly with Grønbech's ideas as expressed in the older four-volume work on old Scandinavian culture. The résumé lacks the stylistic brilliance and the inspiring originality of the seminal work, but it in no way contradicts or alters what Grønbech had written between 1909 and 1912. In fact, it is to a large extent a selection of passages—which to be sure often have been compressed—from *Vor Folkeæt i Oldtiden*. While this resumé is useful only for readers of Danish, the resumé in German included in Chantepie de la Saussaye's *Lehrbuch der Religionsgeschichte* is accessible to a learned, international audience. It is more traditionally historical than Grønbech's magnum opus, makes fewer assumptions regarding the reader's knowledge of Scandinavian antiquity, and also includes a summary of Grønbech's opinions (from the year 1913) regarding the conversion of Scandinavia.

In addition to these several scholarly essays, Grønbech published a volume for popular consumption in which he retold in his own words old Scandinavian myths and tales. The book was first issued in Swedish translation in 1926; the Danish original appeared in 1927 under the title *Nordiske Myter og Sagn (Scandinavian Myths and Tales)*. Here Grønbech was able to make greater use of his penchant for imaginative writing than in his critical and historical works. The demonstration of this facility as a narrator is given by the fact that the book was republished twice in the 1940s and has since 1964 undergone several printings as a paperback. A German translation was published in 1929, republished in 1932, and reprinted in 1943 and 1949. The collection was not a translation from older Scandinavian sources but a retelling in Grønbech's own words of material found in the *Elder Edda*, in the *Edda* of Snorri Sturluson, in the twelfth-century Latin history of Saxo Grammaticus, in certain of the Old Icelandic mythical-heroic sagas, and also in the Old English *Beowulf*.

CHAPTER 3

Defining Our Patrimony

*R*eligious Currents in the Nineteenth Century *(Religiøse strømninger i det nittende aarhundrede)*[1] occupies a central position
in Grønbech's work if only because it stands, so to speak, at the
fulcrum of his production. His first book had been published in
1902, and the last separate book written in his lifetime was published in 1946; *Religious Currents* appeared in 1922. The volume
was produced for a series (edited by Aage Friis) intended to delineate the main cultural currents of the nineteenth century. Grønbech's book did not fully observe the guidelines set by the editor for
the series, in the first place because, for good reason, Grønbech's
concern was roughly with the hundred years between about 1775
and 1875 rather than the nineteenth century *per se*, and in the
second, because he dealt with Germany and England and to a certain extent Scandinavia, but omitted France from consideration—
according to his own testimony because of the limitation of space
imposed by the publisher. That there was no reference to other
European countries such as Italy, Spain, Poland, and Russia must
be interpreted to mean that these countries were not to be considered as progenitors of dominant or new ideas in religion,
philosophy, or science in the era Grønbech was examining.

Religious Currents serves incidentally as an introduction to
Grønbech's later works, several of which are to be found here in
embryo. A general thesis was established and developed in the
book, but several individual chapters were devoted to figures about
whom Grønbech was soon to publish treatises, notably Johann
Gottfried Herder, Johann Wolfgang Goethe, and Friedrich
Schlegel.

Grønbech was one of the earlier critics to agitate for establishing a
new watershed of Western historiography by looking upon the years
around 1770, rather than the Reformation, with its symbolic date

1517, as the beginning of what may more properly be called modern times. While he did not underestimate the significance of the Reformation, he considered the second half of the eighteenth century as constituting the recognizable and important turning point from which our own, modern times could be dated, as is implied in the remark that the death of God occurred about the year 1770. An old established order had grown gradually to a close; in much of Europe the Enlightenment had overcome traditional faith, and rationalism had been accepted within the limitations that the teleological assumption could permit. Yet at this very point, rationalism was discovered not to be sufficient to fill out men's lives. There was a longing for something beyond mere reasoned explanation, or, as Grønbech formulated it, there was a struggle for a new soul. The German *Sturm und Drang*, the grotesque imagination of an E. T. A. Hoffmann, the newly awakened consciousness of the literature of the Scandinavian Middle Ages, a revival of enthusiasm for Greek antiquities (which, however, dated back to Winckelmann), the poetry of Byron, Herder's interest in primitivism—all these were indicative of an attempt to explain the world anew and to achieve understanding and appreciation for an existence beyond the structures of a social order dominated by the dogma of medieval Christianity.

Not only was the phrase "nineteenth century" in the title of the book somewhat inaccurate, as was its coverage of only a part of Western Europe, but the phrase "religious currents" itself might lead a reader to believe that he was about to be confronted with a study that was devoted to ecclesiastical history or religion in the everyday sense of the term: organized religion and its tenets. Not so. Grønbech was endeavoring to illuminate the most poignant forces of the nineteenth century: those ideas that created the metaphysical numinousity in which we exist. Such ideas or currents were for Grønbech identifiable as religious. And he pointed out that in the nineteenth century those currents found expression primarily in imaginative literature and in the new science. The concepts of the nineteenth century which were so nearly fundamental and so important that they could be labeled as articles of religious faith, in that they molded the lives of those who believed in them, had little to do with traditional Christian belief or church dogma, and similarly distanced themselves from the culture of the Renaissance, which was closely joined to late medieval thought and which had provided a

basis for life in the West since the beginning of the sixteenth century. The problems of human existence had found one explanation
in antiquity and another in the Middle Ages; some of those oldest
and older explanations were carried along in a kind of synthesis
within the Renaissance and its metaphysical if not wholly fixed or
stable basis, Christianity, but a new and different explanation was
generated by the poets and scientists of early modern time. Thus,
poets and scientists had in Grønbech's eyes become the religious
leaders of the nineteenth century. They had new experiences; they
can therefore be said to have created the human soul anew; and they
were responsible for the new dominant intellectual and spiritual
currents of the century. Almost two decades later, in the first volume of his study on Hellenism, Grønbech was to write in the same
spirit: "The poet is not only a scientist in verse. He has the great task
of changing the outside world into the material of the soul and by his
example helping other people in their work to sublimate worthless
experiences to worthwhile moods."[2] Curiously enough Grønbech
did not subsume Marxist thought and its gradually evolving dogmatic political components under the heading of religious currents.

In Grønbech's eyes modern times can be characterized as the
search for a new harmony. Earlier established religions were able to
create the myth of a harmony; and Grønbech believed that we now
need to create our own myth if we are to achieve harmony. By myth
Grønbech was not suggesting some arbitrary construction that
might be subject to ridicule but a stable and well-grounded and
well-rounded metaphysical construction that could serve as a basis
for an organized society and life within that society. If we look into
the past we can discern societies that functioned satisfactorily because of the acceptance by the members of the society of a complex
or system of tenets, some of which might be elucidated in the form
of moral lessons, while others were unspoken assumptions of the
same nature as those that Grønbech had endeavored to plumb in his
study of the culture of the Teutons. Several places in his work,
Grønbech mentioned the need for myth in modern society, and in
the volume of essays entitled *Kampen for ny sjæl (The Struggle for a
new Soul)*, which first appeared in Swedish in 1940 and then partially in Danish in 1946, one chapter is titled "Will our century find
its myth?" Only by the acceptance of a myth—that is, a system of
belief—Grønbech implies, can a new harmony be created. By tran-
scending the culture and philosophy of the Renaissance, the men of

the new age had attained much self-knowledge and achieved new spiritual wealth, but "all was chaos: passion and reason were at odds because nothing knew its place or function."[3] Grønbech calls Goethe's *Werther* and Chateaubriand's *René* the heroes of the new generation who feel they have the power to create a new world but later find existence loathful or languorous.

The beginning of Grønbech's book is impressively provocative:

We, the children of the nineteenth century, are a generation without a religion and therefore we have but a single thought: how can we find a god and a devil, a heaven and a hell—all those things which made earlier times great? We know that the old god is dead and gone, and that no attempt at resuscitation can give him back the power and the glory. We can date his departure around the year 1770. He died when men found it necessary to prove his existence; he was buried when they discovered that there was nothing by which his existence was disproved. A god who does not make himself noticed lies dead in his grave; and gods never rise again after the reins of the world have once slipped from their hands.[4]

These words not only expresss Grønbech's conviction, they have associations with the past and with the future, that is, with the proclamations of the German thinker Friedrich Nietzsche as well as the post–World War II theology that propounded the thesis, "God is dead." Such associations are, however, superficial. Closer examination reveals, on the one hand, that Grønbech's intent was philosophically different from Nietzsche's and, on the other, that the motivation for Grønbech's analyses was dissimilar from that of the more recent, gloomy theologians. It is odd that Grønbech does not mention Nietzsche in *Religious Currents*—perhaps for chronological reasons, since Nietzsche's contributions actually were made subsequent to the major clash about the Darwinian theory. Grønbech was certainly aware of Nietzsche for, according to his widow, he was planning at the time of his death to write a book on Nietzsche.

Another striking association and echo is with the early work of Georg Brandes, notably the series of lectures begun in 1871 and later reworked in book form under the title *Main Currents of Nineteenth-Century Literature*. The parallelism between Grønbech and Brandes extends beyond mere words in the title of their books: both stressed the new literature of Germany around 1800 and the new literature of England in the early nineteenth century. Their approaches to these literatures were very different; nevertheless, it is hard to believe that Grønbech did not himself sense the parallelism with Brandes while he was writing *Religious Currents*. The fact that Grønbech did not treat French literature whereas Brandes did has been explained as a space limitation. Grønbech may well have felt that his work was a corrective to that of Brandes, for he was very skeptical of Brandes' modus operandi. He felt that Brandes often passed judgment on the basis of insufficient familiarity with the works in question and that Brandes was a slave to his own aesthetic, pragmatic method. In any case, Grønbech was convinced that Brandes had missed the essential quality of the literature with which he was dealing and had failed to understand that the literature of the nineteenth century, like the new natural science, was the receptacle and the embodiment of the motivating forces of the time.

Grønbech spoke of a generation that had attained new self-knowledge and therefore had decreed a new self and sought a new harmony. In Grønbech's terms the soul was confused and the world chaotic after the anthropocentric Renaissance and its Christian religion lost their hold on intellectuals. The apparent understanding of an harmonious nature governed by laws of justice was swept away, and this meant that human life lost strength and cohesion. There had to be a reordering of thought so that there could be a revised teleological comprehension of the universe and of man's existence within it.

The early efforts for reestablishment of harmony as evidenced in the work of the young Goethe or Chateaubriand were not successful. Grønbech felt that he could identify one prophet around 1800 who pointed to the path that must be taken in the future, however: William Blake. But Blake was not heard in the great confusion of his own time. Grønbech's concern with English literature, which dated from his years as lecturer in English at the University of Copenhagen, also familiarized him with Wordsworth (as it did incidentally with Robert Browning, Dickens, Byron, Shelley, and various other English writers). Grønbech felt that Wordsworth, unlike Shelley, with whom Wordsworth had a sensitivity in common, had indeed achieved harmony. Grønbech's thoughts vis-à-vis Wordsworth had already generated an essay published in 1915 in the Norwegian literary periodical *Edda*, an essay later revised and included in volume IV of Grønbech's *Mystics of Europe and India*.

Grønbech makes much of the discovery of a new reality and even suggests that a new reality might be equated with a rebirth of God. "Compared with this inward experience," he says, "doctrine is inconsequential."[5] After discussing Goethe, Herder, the young Friedrich Schlegel, and Novalis, Grønbech could write, "none of these men was a dreamer, none of them was a questing soul who wandered about looking for something other than reality. What they had found, they had found by living. They had captured eternity in the common day, and they harbored no fantasies about a salvation which one can achieve by mortification and fasting. They found salvation in the actuality of the day. . . ."[6]

Goethe and Herder had been the early champions of the new thought. Although they had been confronted by chaos, Herder had achieved spiritual harmony and Goethe the view of a cosmos. Herder had seen unity beyond multiplicity; Goethe had a vision of the prototype in nature. In their attitudes toward culture, Herder and Goethe differed. Herder was tolerant of all cultural patterns; his was the more modern position. Goethe accepted the "fictitious Greek," as Grønbech puts it, as the ideal: the Hellene was the paragon that should be a model for our time and all time. Grønbech felt that Goethe had capitulated to impatience. Herder, in Grønbech's opinion, had the greater insight of the two, for he was able to dismiss the biases, fixed ideas, and narrowness of historical thinking that hitherto had obtained. "In place of reason or virtue or bliss, as the goal of man's endeavor, he puts *humanity:* the highest form into which a man could mould himself, given the conditions of his time."[7]

Grønbech's great sympathy and predilection for Herder is particularly evident in the chapter entitled "The new God" in *Religious Currents.* Grønbech in some ways can be identified with Herder, and he placed great emphasis on Herder both in *Religious Currents* and also in his lectures at the University of Copenhagen. Regarding Herder, Grønbech wrote: "[F]or Herder all religions are true as long as they incorporate and formulate a people's experience, and religions are valuable to posterity as evidence of those experiences which each of us must undergo anew. Herder cannot accept a religion which is pure speculation or pure morality; for him religion is something man lives into with all his senses; religion embraces the entire man; and to live a religion is to endeavor to ennoble the entire soul."[8] These sentiments seem to be completely in accord with Grønbech's own attitude throughout his *œuvre* and to be in the

spirit of a modern historian of religion. Grønbech further puts into
Herder's mouth a definition of religion to which he himself seems to
have subscribed: "Religion is poetry and myth, the visions of wisdom and the fantasies of fools; it has grown under the adroit supervi-
sion of priests and prophets, and by their crafty exploitation of the
deference of the people. In the myths and pious conventions of
religion, men are united organically with the great events in nature
and in human life; and religion, as it traditionally descends from
father to son and meets the child as he enters into life, acts as a
shield between a man and the outer world, and prevents him from
beginning for himself, face to face with nature."[9]

The young writers around the year 1800, the so-called Romantics,
"expanded their souls," to use Grønbech's phrase, and discovered
"a world replete with latent energy for him who lost himself in
passion."[10] What for the meditative scholar had been closed, sprang
open for ecstatic youth, says Grønbech, because the soul "arrays
itself in nature as if it were an extension of his body. . . . [I]n this
overwhelming experience there occurs a merging of the soul and the
world which casts light both inward and outward."[11] The experience
of passion, Grønbech continues, revealed to the young men "that
there is no line of demarcation between the inner and the outer;
what happens in the soul, occurs in nature; what begins on one side
undulates immediately to the other."[12]

Grønbech points out that for Herder "the spirit reveals itself
gradually throughout history," whereas for the Romantics "the spirit
is equally accessible everywhere, in the landscape as in the human
soul."[13] The inward experiences of the new writers around 1800
distinguished them from Herder and Goethe.

"The Romantics threw a torch to the world, but the world did not
catch it,"[14] Grønbech writes with particular reference to the new
literature of Germany at the beginning of the nineteenth century.
He then undertakes to describe the intellectual climate of Germany
that encouraged the establishment of numerous new disciplines,
including his own, the history of religion, prior to the advent of a
new salvation that was to come from England. Herder and Goethe
are seen as the sources of inspiration for the new literature and the
new disciplines, but the general mood in Germany is one of unrest
and some discouragement because no strong new belief arises.
Grønbech mentions the negative cast of a religious philosophy produced by Schopenhauer and David Friedrich Strauss who on the

one hand described a man's life as a delusion and on the other suggested that satisfaction can be given only by art. He speaks ironically of the efforts of the Grimm brothers to perceive the voice of God in folk literature, which was supposed to express the soul of the people with whom it was identified. Grønbech does not underestimate the importance of the so-called Germanic Renaissance of the early nineteenth century, however, and recognizes that the Grimms gave Germany what it needed: "a relation to the past." Grønbech's irony was peculiarly sharp since Jacob Grimm, like Grønbech, also chose particular words from the Germanic vocabulary on which to establish his theses, albeit in a dilettante fashion wholly unlike Grønbech's method in *The Culture of the Teutons*. Grønbech calls special attention to the awareness of the religions of India that first came about through writings of Friedrich Schlegel and more particularly of Max Müller, although Müller and his school failed to realize that the subject with which they dealt so pragmatically was in fact what Grønbech identified as the mightiest force in the world: religion.

No slight advance was the discovery or rediscovery of Eros and the recognition of the beauty and the power of attraction between man and woman, which is symbolic of the desire to embrace the unknown. "Their play is energetic and painful because a greater force is playing through them. In the two human beings the dynamic soul of nature rises to the surface; the two feel that they form a universe struggling to become conscious of itself, for they partake of the same soul and the same pain that strive in nature to break out of the conscious life of plants and to surge upward from form to form."[15] Grønbech is here clearly alluding to Novalis and the erotically charged *Hymnen an die Nacht*.

Grønbech saw in the new literature around 1800—a literature most frequently identified as Romantic—the proclamation of a religion of the future; the word "God" was informed with new meaning: "every man has his own god in the ideal which lives in him and which through his life he makes into reality."[16] In connection with this remark Grønbech observed that in the case of Schleiermacher at least the belief in a personal God was not necessarily part of true religion. The relation of the Romantics to existing religion Grønbech described as "enlightened rejection," since they do not accept the "absolute sobriety, pure morals, complete self-abnegation" of Protestantism and demand instead passion, ecstasy, and myths—"myths

such as the great man of Nazareth once created."[17] "And the principal commandment is that man should live according to his abundance, be completely himself, and in so doing live completely for
others."[17]

In England the new movement is identified with Thomas Carlyle,
John Stuart Mill, and, above all, the Darwinian doctrine of evolution. Grønbech speaks of Huxley and Darwin in terms that are
traditionally religious. He says, for example, "Darwin and Huxley
are culturally related to the Israelites who demanded a God who was
just with the justice of Israel, only more unsparing and clearer of
vision; and of course this spiritual relationship is no accident."[18] Just
at the time when the metaphysical unity of traditional religion was
being eroded and, as a consequence, the implicit belief in goodness
and justice appeared to be without foundation, succor came. When
the need was greatest, science provided the solution. The views of
Spencer and Darwin regarding the construction and evolution of the
world actually permitted a new teleology to be established through
which one could again perceive a system of the existence of justice
and goodness, although Grønbech makes clear that we must now
seek our bases in history. "The ethics of harmony," he says, "are
reborn in the concept of evolution."[19] The old ideals gained stability
and power by becoming independent of human commands and divine threats, and by being based solely on the law of nature."[20]
"Evolution," he continued, "met actuality on its own territory,
sought God within experience, and found him in laws. With a ruth-
less love of truth, it dismissed all attempts to improve actuality by
the use of the imagination; mercilessly it brushed away the withered
leaves in which earlier generations had clad their experiences, and
then provided a rational costume for experience."[21] Above all,
evolution is the religious expression of the nineteenth century, as
Grønbech entitled chapter 12 of *Religious Currents*. "Evolution,"
he avers, "represents the rebirth of the religion of harmony in a
purified form,"[22] for the evolutionists possessed a "triumphant
faith" in the laws of nature and their adequacy. In this they shared a
belief with those who accepted God as creator and maintainer and "a
symbol of the dominance of law in nature."

In *Religious Currents*, Grønbech makes the point that churchmen
and evolutionists actually shared a common belief in the planned
order of the universe. "In evolution," wrote Grønbech, "the church
met itself without knowing it. Blindly eager to attack a presumed

enemy, the church did not discover until later that it had wounded itself every time it struck."[23] Grønbech explained that the church lagged behind because it defended the religion of the Renaissance, which no longer conformed to actuality. "But," Grønbech notes, "actuality could not be outwitted."[24] Ultimately the church found its solace, Grønbech continues, "in the immutability of nature, its perfect order, and its ethical harmony." This was, of course, parallel to the cognition of the doctrine of evolution.

Grønbech was amused by the parallels that could be drawn between the doctrine of evolution and the official Christian religion. He writes: "The crux of the matter was this: the scholar and the Christian were in agreement on all significant points. The most pious churchman could not express his faith in the planned order of the universe more eloquently than the heretical evolutionist. There was no difference from sacred oratory when such unordained men as Darwin and Huxley spoke about the lofty ideals of humanity, about ethical responsibility and firmness in self-denial. . . . The most pious of the pious could not be more inexorable than Huxley in his assertion of the traditional virtues of purity, compassion, justice, and truth."[25]

With an ironical bit of self-observation, Grønbech commented that evolution itself had created a new and better theology—the name of which is the history of religion; and, he continued, "the history of religion should above all explain the dreadful fact that man has made his own religions, and that often he has made himself a religion that seems barbaric or insane."[26]

In concluding *Religious Currents,* Grønbech struck an optimistic note by saying, "A new harmony must be found and it will be found. But whether the new times will make use of the old forms, religious and social, or whether they will weave a new garment for experience, no one knows."[27] And harmony, Grønbech had stated earlier in the book, "gives a man security, for he knows that he has only to allow wise nature to have its way with man in society; he need only give the individual the freedom to participate in the struggle—and society will be well served. Correctly understood, all virtues are compounded of pure, noble egoism."[28]

CHAPTER 4

Probing the Mystics

I A Paradox

BETWEEN 1925 and 1934 Grønbech published four books with
the series' title *Mystikere i Europa og Indien (Mystics in
Europe and India)*. The first volume dealt with the religions of
India; a notable section of the book (published separately after
Grønbech's death) was devoted to Buddha. The second volume con-
tained three essays, one on Heraclitus, one on Meister Eckehart,
and one on Ruysbroek. Volume III was devoted solely to Theresa de
Jesus; volume IV again contained three essays: on John Donne,
Wordsworth, and the German thinker Johann Gottfried Herder.
Not all of the figures about whom Grønbech was writing—namely,
Wordsworth and Herder—would ordinarily be considered mystics.
The selection was nevertheless not arbitrary. If Wordsworth and
Herder were not imbued with mystical experience in the traditional
sense of the term, then they had experienced the unity of existence,
each in his own way: a unity of the human being and his natural
surroundings comparable to the mystic's innermost feeling of union
with the supernatural. With one exception, the mystics about whom
Grønbech was writing evoked his respect. The exception was Ruysbroek, against whom Grønbech, at least verbally, expressed no less
than antipathy. Here as elsewhere, however, Grønbech was able to
identify himself with his subject in such a manner that one does not
realize that there could be a complete lack of spiritual affinity between author and subject. In addition to the four volumes incorpo-
rated into the series, Grønbech in 1933 published a book on William
Blake that in its subtitle identified Blake as a mystic.

It is paradoxical that Grønbech, who was a champion of a shared
faith and the necessity for an individual to feel that he belonged to a
community of believers, concerned himself at such length with mys-
50

tics who by definition have a personal relationship with the supernatural and are unable to share their experiences. There are at least
two reasons that help explain this paradox. First, Grønbech felt that
the mystics about whom he was writing were *per se* important and
influential in the history of the human spirit and were among those
human beings who had sensed the existence of more than a single
reality. Second, there is convincing autobiographical evidence that
Grønbech himself once had what can be identified as a mystical
experience. This does not mean that one can pin on Grønbech the
permanent label of mystic, but according to his own testimony he
had such a sensation at some time during the first few years of the
century. By 1910, however, he had taken a detached and objective
attitude toward mystics and mysticism. Nevertheless, because of his
own experience, he was able to write with understanding and sympathy about mystics from a position that was now one of disinterest.
In a paraphrase of Herder, Grønbech says: "Mysticism has been
useful because it has drawn men's minds away from the empty and
superstitious ceremonies of the church, taught them to look into
themselves and given them spiritual pabulum, but fortunately those
times when this opium was necessary as medicine are now past."[1]
The word opium in this connection might seem to echo Karl Marx,
but was in fact taken directly from Herder.

In the introduction to a popular anthology of mystical writing
which Vilhelm Grønbech and Aage Marcus edited in 1929, Grønbech states: "The word mysticism has been misused to such a degree that it is in danger of becoming meaningless. Many people,
both learned and unlearned, use it as a sack in which to collect
everything that goes beyond their own practical experience; one can
hear a man called mystic because he believes . . . that there are
more things in heaven and earth than the philosophers have dreamt
of."[2] Grønbech then provides the beginning of a definition: "A mystic is a man who has discovered a world beyond that in which
everyday people live, another existence, where mortals are elevated
above all the longings and desires which under the conditions of this
earthly life not infrequently are damaged or destroyed in the struggle against fate." Grønbech was not agitating for mysticism but
rather for an understanding of the phenomenon of mysticism. Some
mystics, and particularly Saint Theresa, he looked upon as having
had positive and practical influence upon their surroundings and
upon posterity, although other mystics, and particularly Ruysbroek,

were selfish and contributed little or nothing to their fellow men. The general observation underlying all his studies of mystics Grønbech enunciated in his short work on the conversion of Scandinavia, published in 1913: "The current of mysticism which rises and falls through the last few millenia is not identical with any church or any religion."[3]

II   Indian Mysticism

The beginning of the volume entitled *Indisk mystik* (*Indian Mysticism*, 1925) is difficult reading. Moreover, the section on the *Upanishads* paraphrases the Indian texts without making clear just what is paraphrase, what is quotation, and what is Grønbech's own formulation. The explanation for this curious beginning is to be sought in the fact that the first part of the volume originally was published in the annual of the University of Copenhagen. Grønbech had something of a different audience in mind than when, later the same year, he united the original academic publication with his more general interpretation of Indian religion and in particular his treatment of Buddha. The parts of the book are very different. If the treatment of the *Upanishads* is not easily grasped, then his remarks about Yoga and the entire second chapter about the Indian attitude toward life are readily comprehensible. And Grønbech writes with considerably more enthusiasm about Vedic religion than the other religions that he describes, presumably because he saw in it a religion of harmony.

Indian Mysticism is a general introduction to the principal religions of India. Grønbech takes his reader by the hand, as it were, and introduces him one after the other to the *Upanishads*, to Vedanta, to Bhakti, and then presents him with a lengthy discourse on the Buddha, which is in turn followed by chapters on Indian eroticism (the term is slightly misleading out of its religious context) and on Krishna. The work is investigative and interpretive in the broad sense of those terms.

Grønbech does not write about Indian religions because he wants to convince his reader; there is no desire to introduce some principles of Indian religion into the West. He is attempting rather to understand the psyche as affected by the most potent forces that play upon the lives of millions of people. If we are to understand our fellow men who live in cultures other than our own, then some comprehension of their innermost convictions as expressed in religion is a necessity: this is a practical tenet of the historian and the student of religion. The historian of religion serves us as a guide into the spiritual areas which seem dark and unfathomable to those who have not familiarized themselves with the sources and who do not know the languages in which the monuments of another religion are preserved.

A second reason for concerning oneself with the religions of India—or the religions of any culture—is that they in themselves constitute an interesting human phenomenon. The humanist believes that every creation of the human spirit is worthy of investigation and study, and a man's beliefs and the rules by which he lives—whether conscious or subconscious—are the basis upon which every other action evolves. The study and comprehension of religions warrants first place among all serious investigations that would answer the question, What is life?—and its corollary, How is life to be lived?

A third reason that Vilhelm Grønbech was attracted to the religions of India as a subject for investigation subsequent to his thorough examination of the religious concepts of the Germanic peoples was the parallelism perceived between certain Indian religions or religious ideas on the one hand and West European Christianity on the other. Specifically, the Bhakti religion, which combines mysticism with the public worship of a God, presents a parallel to Christianity. As Grønbech discusses the other religions of India, the theology of Vedanta, the doctrine of love in Krishna, and the psychology in Buddha's teachings, the reader himself senses numerous similarities within his own religious culture and as a consequence grows more critical toward his own beliefs. In an essay "On the Position of Scholarship in Public Life" from the year 1912, Vilhelm Grønbech mentions twentieth-century European interest in India and explains it as an instinctive feeling that self-abnegation is the only way to save the inner life of an individual. We begin to understand, he says, that the cult and myth of the Orient express an intense relationship to nature that is more lasting than the Western enthusiasm for wild and unpeopled woods and mountains.

Grønbech has acquainted himself with the source material of the Indian religions and, upon finding them worthy of attention, conveys the ideas of these religions to his countrymen in his own words. As previously discussed, he uses the paraphrase extensively, particularly in his treatment of the *Upanishads,* so that for the uninitiated reader it is impossible to distinguish between Grønbech and the sources he is citing. This fact makes the reading less rather than more difficult, since Grønbech is simplifying complex abstractions and making an effort to enable his reader to grasp a completely different *Weltanschauung* than that with which the reader is familiar and temporarily to accept a different approach to existence.

As in *The Culture of the Teutons* and later in the work *Hellas*, Grønbech frequently employs untranslated terms that are significant in the religious culture of which he is speaking, in the case of India notably the concepts of *karma* and *atman*. He does not use such terms casually, however, and does make an endeavor to define and explain them. Thus, for example, his definition of *karma* begins: "*karma* means first and foremost an unbroken unity in life; each act directly generates its successor."[4] He continues with extensions and variations of his definition at some length until the reader is able, if only by a process of delimitation, to grasp the concept that Grønbech would interpret.

In his earlier works Grønbech had evinced admiration for the harmony of existence as found in the religion of a community of believers. The Indian religions of which he writes are attractive to him when he finds in them the achievement of harmony and the active participation of believers in religious activity, notably in ritual and festival. At the beginning of his book he describes Indian mythology as a metaphysical construct, but he writes in unbiased and wholly sympathetic terms. The mythology is felt to be a necessary projection of the human comprehension of existence. In speaking of the hymns of the *Rigveda*, Grønbech explains that one can perceive that the culture that produced them was harmonious—and natural. He then explains his terms. By "natural" he means that the activities and the spiritual life of the people held to the rhythm of nature and received their inspiration directly from such alternation as summer and winter, growth and drought, fertility and lean years; by "harmony" he means that the people created a whole in which social institutions comprise the expression of collective labor and a feeling of communality. One observes immediately that these are characteristics shared by the ancient Germanic people as depicted in *The Culture of the Teutons*. In Grønbech's *Hellas*, similar characteristics are identified in classical antiquity. As in *The Culture of the Teutons*, Grønbech stresses in *Indian Mysticism* the creative quality of the religious festival and its virtue as a preservative of traditional culture. The festival, he writes, was a time of rebirth when God and man functioned in sacred unity, so that blessings flowed upward as well as downward.

A parallel may be drawn between Grønbech's treatment of Buddha in 1925 and his treatment of Jesus a decade later. In both cases he was convinced that the words ascribed to the master and which have been preserved were indeed genuine, primarily because he felt no one else would have been in a position to speak such words. This is, of course, a matter of opinion and cannot be demonstrated. In both cases Grønbech is concerned with the figure of the religious leader and not with the religion that arose on the basis of his teachings. Grønbech is also giving a personal interpretation, for his Buddha is not the all-embracing religious figure to which one could point in order to explain the widespread appeal of Buddhism in the world. Grønbech presents Buddha as an upper class man who had little understanding for the realities of life and who had little social consciousness. This observation in particular distinguishes Buddha from Buddhism.

It had been apparent in *The Culture of the Teutons* that Grønbech was partisan insofar as he expressed admiration for the existence of religious harmony, since religious harmony led also to a life of harmony. He looked back to Germanic antiquity and sensed a time when society had enjoyed harmony because its members shared a set of compatible beliefs. Although Grønbech is often critical of Buddha on the one hand and Buddhism on the other (and he points out at various times that the two cannot be equated any more than Jesus Christ can be equated with Christianity as it developed after His death), he senses that a harmony of the soul can be achieved by following the tenets of Buddha. Grønbech's attitude toward Buddha is thus ambivalent insofar as he categorizes Buddha as a mystic. And Budda is a mystic, for the way that he points to harmony goes through the individual. This is the mystic's way. Subsequent to his own mystical experience at the beginning of the twentieth century, Grønbech looked upon the mystic as selfish in emphasizing solely his own relationship to the supernatural. Grønbech explains that Buddha's concern was with the salvation of the individual soul—a characteristic that Buddha must be said to have held in common with Grønbech's *bête noir*, Søren Kierkegaard. One infers that Grønbech could not accept Buddha's teaching, for it was on this point that Grønbech disagreed so strongly with Kierkegaard. Buddha is interesting because of his emphasis upon rules of conduct and ethics, however. According to Buddha, Grønbech points out, the harmony of the soul is won only by constant self-education and self-discipline, and Buddha, of all the religious leaders, is the one for whom there is but one life, this life on earth, although he despises worldliness. In a paradoxical sentence, Grønbech says that Buddha is in reality fighting mystics with mysticism.[5]

III   Heraclitus. Eckehart. Ruysbroek.

With the second volume *Mystics in Europe and India*, Grønbech moves from India to Europe, but without attempting to write any systematic or unified essay. Volume II (1932) is in three disparate sections, the first on Heraclitus of Ephesos, the Greek thinker who lived in the fifth century B. C.; the second on Meister Echehart, the best known German mystic, who lived in the thirteenth and early fourteenth century; and the third on Jan de Ruysbroek, the Netherlandic mystic who was a contemporary of Meister Eckehart.

Heraclitus, said Vilhelm Grønbech, is immortal on the basis of a handful of quotations. The Ephesian seems early to have captured his imagination; the handful of quotations was sufficient for Grønbech to be drawn to him repeatedly in an effort to identify the harmony for which Heraclitus seems to be the speaker. It is a curious fact that Grønbech addressed himself to Heraclitus no fewer than four times in his *œuvre*. Grønbech first wrote about Heraclitus in the yearbook of the Lund Academy of Sciences in 1929. This essay, which was in essence an exposition of the fragments of the Greek thinker, was reworked for inclusion in volume II of *Mystics in Europe and India*. Subsequently, Grønbech wrote about Heraclitus in the work *Hellas*, and then returned to him once more in lectures given in 1943–44 in Copenhagen but published posthumously under the title *Lyset fra Akropolis* (*The Light from the Acropolis*, 1951).

The beginning of the essay on Heraclitus is a stimulating historical synthesis that finds a parallel in the introduction to Grønbech's volume on Paul. Grønbech writes that Heraclitus, "lived in a fateful time when all thoughts and all forms were in the melting pot. In these centuries Greece was shaken by a political crisis the origins of which are to be found in severe social and economic problems. The old society that had arisen on the basis of the patriarchal, localized culture was about to explode because of economic revolutions that created a new, more flexible and supple type of man, the merchant."[6] Heraclitus belonged to the established order, however, and Grønbech dubs him "the old aristocrat." Heraclitus was a speaker for an ideal culture that once had existed in honor and idealism. Grønbech admires Heraclitus because he represented a culture that believed it had achieved eternal harmony and that had an awareness of the eternal.

Grønbech senses in Heraclitus a well-rounded world pattern and a union between the mundane and the divine. He stresses Heraclitus' metaphor of fire as the eternal and all-embracing reality and twice quotes the words that "God is day and night, winter and summer, war and peace, plenty and want."[7] Grønbech perceives a unity in Heraclitus' fragmentary ideas—a unity of the universe that combines the supernatural with the natural. For this reason Grønbech considers Heraclitus a mystic who could be mentioned together with Meister Eckehart and Ruysbroek—with whom he shares volume II of *Mystikere.*

Grønbech viewed Meister Eckehart as the most important mystic of the Middle Ages in Western civilization for several reasons. Presumably most significant is the observation that Eckehart was able to create a reality of his own, a metaphysical existence within the strictures of traditional theological Christianity but at the same time autonomous and resting upon its own assumptions. A second reason is that Eckehart's teachings have a certain metaphysical purity lacking in many other thinkers of the Middle Ages in that he is, as Grønbech puts it, free of legend and myth. It is possible to divine a structure of his thought without having to dismiss large segments of it as foreign or irrelevant. A third reason is the fact that Eckehart wrote much of his work in his native German tongue. He wanted to speak not only to fellow theologians but also to the layman in order to transmit his understanding of the existence of the soul, the existence of God, and the equation of soul and God that he perceived. Finally, Eckehart is significant to Grønbech because Grønbech feels that Eckehart harbored a modern conviction of the anthropocentricity of the concept of God, or, to speak somewhat more crudely, of the metaphysical existence of God having been created by the mind of man. Grønbech uses the phrase "his time's God." While he does not elaborate upon this phrase, Grønbech's mere use of it permits us to conclude that for Grønbech God was a shifting concept—which, of course, does not exclude the existence of constants within the dynamic concept.

If one looks at the list of chapter headings and subheadings in Grønbech's essay on Eckehart, one assumes that Grønbech has created a rationally organized presentation and convincing argument regarding Eckehart's thought. In fact, that is not the case. Except for introductory comments about Eckehart's life and for biographical intercalations in the essay, Grønbech is essentially paraphrasing Eckehart. The wealth of abstraction and metaphor that is found in Eckehart is reborn in Grønbech, so that his essay is no more a convincing single argument or a lucid interpretation than is Eckehart himself. While Grønbech may be said to synthesize Eckehart's thoughts, he has not done so so that the reader is given a few simple judgments that can be assumed to characterize Eckehart.

"Eckehart leads us inward into ourselves and shows us the true life of the soul,"[8] Grønbech writes, and this is one observation that can be borne in mind. It does not follow, however, that one will find a simple key to the life of the soul any more than that there is a simple key to the interpretation of the universe. Grønbech's intent was to make Eckehart accessible to the modern reader by modernizing Eckehart's language without modernizing his metaphysics. The result is nevertheless demanding and even tiring today, in part because of the lack of clarity, which is Eckehart's; in part because of his perorations; and in part because of the density of metaphor. Grønbech himself characterizes Eckehart's style with a metaphor taken from Eckehart by calling it a style that "blooms and shoots new leaves." Despite the apparent contradictions in Eckehart, Grønbech insists that Eckehart is basically without paradox and that there is nothing accidental in his language. The peculiarities of Eckehart's language Grønbech explains as a result of the effort to express a reality that belongs on another plane by using the vocabulary of a different reality and a vocabulary burdened with unwanted associations.

Grønbech feels that the church's accusation of heresy against Eckehart was unwarranted, and Grønbech even labels him a true son of the church who could not be revolutionary. Nevertheless, the objection may be raised to Grønbech's interpretation in this connection that the papal bull against Eckehart from the year 1329, which specifically condemns a series of theses that are ascribed to Eckehart, is in fact a good introduction to the ideas that inform Eckehart's work, although today theologians presumably acknowledge Eckehart's view as more nearly valid than the objections raised to them six centuries ago. Viewed historically, Eckehart was not unique but was rather a voluble and enthusiastic spokesman for the direction that theological metaphysics was taking in the later Middle Ages.

In the Eckehart essay, Grønbech takes a curiously unscholarly stance in his notes through his ambivalent position toward secondary literature dealing with Eckehart (prior to 1932) and in particular with regard to the use of a modern German translation of the original Middle High German texts, for it has come to light that the modern translation that Grønbech used is not always accurate. Grønbech's point is well taken, however, that scholars should not dismiss translations of important documents that they either cannot read in the original or can read only with great difficulty. This attitude he felt was one of snobbishness which served only to broaden the gap between scholar and reading public.

Although Grønbech could not identify Eckehart as a rebel within the church, he readily admittted that Eckehart's sermons contained a dangerous element for, although they were not meant to be an attack on the existing order, they could plant doubt in the listener's or reader's mind and therefore subsequently be responsible for a revolution in the structure of metaphysical concepts that were accepted at that time.

The last sixty pages of the second volume of *Mystics* is a grand paraphrase of the enthusiastic reflections and imagery of the fourteenth century Dutch mystic Jan van Ruysbroek. Ruysbroek is much more the traditional egocentric mystic than was Eckehart, and Grønbech expresses considerable surprise that the church was willing to condemn Eckehart but left Ruysbroek unscathed. To anyone who has been made aware of Grønbech's conviction that man's salvation lies in the sharing of a common belief and in the participation of the individual in a community of believers, it is apparent that Ruysbroek represents almost the antithesis of Grønbech's religious ideal. Grønbech is nevertheless able to reformulate Ruysbroek's ideas on the basis of a thorough knowledge of Ruysbroek's works and a reordering of his thoughts into a series of categories that Grønbech apparently feels are indicative of the most important recurrent

ideas which inform Ruysbroek's writing. Curiously enough, Grønbech is able to articulate Ruysbroek in a tone that approaches the
lyric-poetic and conveys something of the intensity of feeling characteristic of the Dutch mystic.

To our post-Freudian generation, much of Ruysbroek's imagery
seems to be derived from sexual repression. Love of God is the
predominant and recurrent concept in Ruysbroek, but his experience of this love is quite as erotic as it is abstractly spiritual. Ruysbroek continually entertains a burning sense of voluptuousness or a
feeling of intoxication in his vision of the divine embrace. The intensity of his love of God transcends all reason as he is overcome with
bodily sensations of longing and sweetness and passion and as he
strives for and senses the indescribable union with the divine. Sentence after sentence and paragraph after paragraph of Grønbech's
paraphrase permit the reader to appreciate the qualities and the
intensity of Ruysbroek's feelings. One cannot help being astonished
at the emotional continuum that is identifiable in Ruysbroek—but
also Grønbech's ability to identify himself with him as a means of
presentation and interpretation of an extreme example of a European mystic. Grønbech is able to inculcate into the reader's mind an
impression of Ruysbroek's ecstasy. His own objectivity is not quite
brushed aside, however, for we find that he identifies Ruysbroek's
writings as constituting an *ars amatoria* that scarcely has its equal.[9]

The comparison between Eckehart and Ruysbroek is not original
with Grønbech; there are several reasons that they have been and
should be compared. They were contemporaries; they were both
mystics; and Ruysbroek passed—negative—judgment on Eckehart.

IV   Theresa de Jesus

Although Grønbech has drawn extensively upon the writings of
Theresa de Jesus for volume III of *The Mystics of Europe and India*,
the book is much more a biography concerned with outward events
than the other essays in the same series. It is evident that Grønbech
was attracted to Theresa and saw in her not only an unusual and able
woman but also a clever and even witty one, as well as a mystic. The
book shares a common weakness with several of Grønbech's other
works in that it is lengthy and reduplicative. This fact, coupled with
the lack of Danish interest in Roman Catholicism and its saints,
accounts for the general disinterest with which the book was met
and the small amount of critical attention paid to it upon publication

and later. The book is nevertheless a masterpiece in its own way, for Grønbech does recreate Theresa in the mind of the reader as an able and very human saint. One of the very few Danes in a position to judge the book when it appeared was Dr. Holger Brøndsted, who was himself an authority on Spanish culture. It is noteworthy that he praised the book both as a scholarly and a popular presentation and noted in particular its "brilliant literary qualities"—but was justifiably skeptical about the book's chances to appeal to the reading public.[10]

If one takes the trouble to read Grønbech on Theresa, one discovers immediately that Grønbech is familiar with every iota of Theresa's own production (although he seems to have depended to a large extent upon English translations of the works, as he himself intimates[11]). From her works Grønbech is able to synthesize a figure who seems credible and comprehensible and whose accomplishments in daily life were quite as important as her thoughts. He presents her as an egocentric, passionate, and coquettish woman who, while ascribing her important decisions to divine inspiration and considering her works to be dedication to God, is always convinced of her own rectitude and the ultimate desirability of all her actions. Grønbech's attitude is felt to be not a little ironic. Grønbech describes Theresa as what now might be identified as a managerial type, although in 1932 he could not have known the term with its modern connotations. Her organizational and operational capacity permitted her to overcome all obstacles that might have prevented her from accomplishing the reformation of the Carmelite order which she undertook and which led to the establishment of some eighteen new houses in Spain during her lifetime and as a result of her own inspiration, labor, intercession, and persuasion.

Theresa is an unusual figure because she is both practical and a mystic, just as for her there was a discrepancy between reality and truth. Her mysticism is at least in part put in the service of practicality. It is apparent that Grønbech felt that Theresa was exploiting the willingness of others to believe in her unusual good fortune in obtaining grace. Although Theresa was ready always to call herself a sinner, Grønbech points out that we know of no sins of which she might be accused and that, according to her testimony, the Lord seemed always to be at her beck and call. As a mystic she was an individualist, as all mystics are, but her individualism became creative, just as her mysticism did not separate her from either ecclesiastical or temporal activity. Grønbech writes about Theresa with considerable ironic humor. He appears often to be speaking tongue-in-cheek and makes his reader feel that Theresa, too, must sometimes have written tongue-in-cheek. Actual Christian humility does not give the impression of having been predominant in Theresa; her remarks about other people are sometimes derogatory and cutting, and the innermost opinions that she seems to have held about not a few of her male superiors were not particularly charitable. In fact, Grønbech writes that a depiction of "Theresa's inner and outer life necessarily is an unbroken series of illustrations of her holy irony and malice."[12] Grønbech calls her a heretic—but a heretic of orthodox faith. He contrasts her with Eckehart and Ruysbroek—to her advantage. Grønbech does not deny, however, that Theresa actually was a mystic and that she did experience religious ecstasy as we can conclude on the basis of her writings.

Grønbech suggests that she did have some characteristics in common with Ruysbroek and in particular in the erotic overtones of her religious enthusiasm. She too felt the need for love and the hunger for satisfaction that she sought in her devotional dedication to God. As in Ruysbroek's case, the modern reader is tempted to label her emotional experience the consequence of sexual repression. The tremendous energy that Theresa expended in her activities as a reformer and as a founder of new cloisters and monasteries can be explained as an alternative to the normal relationships which she did not have. Her struggles to achieve her goals were, as Grønbech puts it, "a time of blossoming for her love life."[13] Her love was of God and she sensed that God requited that love. She could "feel love's jubilation and sweetness permeate all her senses."[14]

For all the admiration that Grønbech can evoke for Theresa as an organizer and as an author, he feels obliged also to express his basic skepticism toward her position, for, in his opinion, "Theresa stood in the middle of a revolution which drew the human being out of his church's communality and transformed him into an individual in his own right who set aside authority for the sake of the voice of the heart."[15] Grønbech thus felt that Theresa was a forerunner of those prophets of the eighteenth century who are our spiritual forefathers and who helped further to demolish a society of believers whose faith was both impelling and cohesive. She quietly undermined the authority she was appealing to, Grønbech concluded, so that although she was not trying to topple the church of which she considered herself to be a true daughter, she was ultimately more dangerous for the future of the church than either Eckehart or Ruysbroek.

V Donne. Wordsworth. Herder

Grønbech's essay on John Donne, which comprises the first part of volume IV of the series on mystics, is an extreme example of Grønbech's paraphrastic method of writing. It not only is impossible to distinguish between Grønbech and his subject much of the time, but it is impossible to determine which poem is being discussed without having access to the text of Donne's poetry—and preferably the same edition that Grønbech used.

Curiously enough, Donne seems to share a characteristic with Ruysbroek in that Grønbech is not sympathetically inclined toward him despite the fact that he elects to write about Donne and seems even to identify himself with Donne in discussing the poetry. Grønbech felt Donne was important because Donne was a paradoxical and an aesthetic poet who could be looked upon as the forerunner of much modern poetry, but this does not mean that Grønbech admired him as a human being. Donne's attitude toward woman would be enough to repel Grønbech who, as we shall learn, was a champion of women's rights, and for whom a woman was not a sex symbol.

While it may seem unexpected that Vilhelm Grønbech wrote on Donne, Wordsworth, and Blake in his studies of mystics (although the book on Blake is not a volume in the series on *Mystics in India and Europe*), we recall that Grønbech had instructed in English literature at the University of Copenhagen between 1908 and 1911. An earlier version of his study on Wordsworth had appeared in the Norwegian periodical *Edda* in 1915. If only for chronological reasons, the essay on Wordsworth may be looked upon as a bridge between *The Culture of the Teutons* and *Mystics*. In *The Culture of the Teutons*, Grønbech had endeavored to ascertain and describe the harmony of metaphysical existence for the Germanic peoples in the pre-Christian era. He described it by identifying its elements as contained in what might today in the terminology of linguists be called the "deep structure" of its metaphysical prerequisites as represented by a set of ideas verbalized in certain key words.

In Wordsworth Grønbech saw an individual who had achieved

harmony within his own metaphysical world. Since Wordsworth was
at one with creation, and creation could be identified as the work of
God, Wordsworth might be called a mystic. Unlike other mystics,
however, Wordsworth was able to express his feelings and to articulate what for the traditional mystic is ineffable. In *The Culture of the
Teutons*, Grønbech had concerned himself with the soul—but the
soul insofar as it was related to a community of believers; in the case
of Wordsworth, however, it was an individual soul that interested
Grønbech. For Grønbech, Wordsworth was one of the greatest of
poets because he had achieved harmony, he could express his spirit
in poetry, and he was at one with nature. Whether Grønbech went
into matters of diction, syntax, and imagery when he dealt with
Wordsworth and other English poets in his tenure as a teacher of
English at the University of Copenhagen is a matter of conjecture.
The details of poetic form were, in any case, not of primary significance to him—as one concludes in examining Grønbech's own
poetry, which is emotionally charged but seems to disregard metri-
cal tradition. Vilhelm Grønbech was no Wordsworth, but Grønbech's poetry, like Wordsworth's poetry, was an expression of that
metaphysical abstraction we call soul.

Grønbech wrote again of Wordsworth in *The Religious Currents
in the Nineteenth Century* in 1922. Here Grønbech explained that
Wordsworth "had learned that the depths of the soul, which expand mysteriously in silent hours, are wealthier than the consciousness, the common light of day, and he remained quiet so that these
depths might speak to him in their power."[16] "Experiences," Grønbech continued, "must be transmuted to wealth in the depths there
where the soul is not a chaos but an incessantly shaping energy."
Grønbech felt that religious formulae were not applicable to
Wordsworth, and that ecstasy, vision, the inner light, or the inner
sense, were all futile phrases when used regarding Wordsworth's
experience.

Grønbech's own enthusiasm for Wordsworth led to the employ-
ment of an imagery that is both poetic and oblique. A reader finds
Grønbech's own metaphorical language stimulating, without, however, being able to reduce his words to a simplistic formulation.
Consider, for example, the two sentences, "He has constructed his
harmony on a new basis, of which the radices lead down to the
depths of the earth, even though he rejoices to include as much as

possible of the walls of the old house above the ground. The older harmony still has sufficient power to sooth and bind him so that he is not perturbed by any recognition that the new life requires new forms."[17]

Some of Grønbech's most profound and inspired writing is found in this essay on Wordsworth which was a revaluation of the poet. In 1922 Grønbech felt that Wordsworth was spiritually most closely related to Goethe and Friedrich Schlegel. Wordsworth had nevertheless sensed "the immediate reality of experience," as Grønbech puts it in quoting Wordsworth's words; he had "felt a presence that disturbs me with the joy of elevated thoughts"— words that were taken from "Lines Composed a few Miles above Tintern Abbey." Grønbech speaks about Wordsworth in such an understanding and familiar fashion that one concludes that he must have found himself in Wordsworth at one time. There is here perhaps a connection with Grønbech's mystical experience at the beginning of the century. In any case, Grønbech wanted also to make it clear to his readers that there were various kinds of mystics; they did not necessarily all resemble Meister Eckehart or Saint Theresa.

Of the various thinkers, writers, and teachers who enjoyed Grønbech's attention and respect and whom he thought to be worthy of emulation, none was more important than the eighteenth century German theologian, cultural historian, and folklorist Johann Gottfried Herder, for with Herder Grønbech shared the most intimate and sympathetic understanding. There are sufficient parallels between Herder and Grønbech for Grønbech to have been termed a Danish Herder. Both men were willing to accept various cultures on their own terms and, as it were, build bridges between cultures rather than attempting a sort of superimposition of the one upon the other. "Herder," writes Grønbech, "ridicules all the historical ideals of his times: the happy belief in the excellence of one's own culture, the belief in progress and in the deity of progress."[18] These are indeed also Grønbech's convictions. As Grønbech says in reflecting on Herder, the course of history is not directed toward a certain culture "but serves a continuous expansion of the possibilities of the soul."[19] Both Herder and Grønbech were concerned with the literature of primitive peoples. Both sought a harmony in human existence and looked abroad for examples of such harmony. Both talked a great deal about the soul, by which they meant both the soul of the individual and the soul of a community of believers or a nation.

Grønbech was of the opinion that Herder's most important single work was *Vom Erkennen und Empfinden der menschlichen Seele (On the Cognition and Feeling of the Human Soul)*, of which an early version was published in 1774 and the final version in 1778. Grønbech felt that all of Herder's later production could be identified embryonically in this work. It is apparent, however, that Grønbech received more inspiration than factual information from Herder; indeed, in may be that Grønbech used Herder more as a point of departure than a source of repeated inspiration. In any case he looked upon Herder as the father of modern history—a discipline that did not fail to take psychological problems into consideration. It was probably not unimportant to Grønbech that Herder was himself a clergyman, although his views when considered in retrospect are considerably at odds with church dogma. In Grønbech's eyes, Herder was a thoroughgoing deist.

One is mildly surprised to find that Grønbech's essay on Herder is included in the series *Mystics in India and Europe,* for ordinarily Herder would scarcely be classified as a mystic. The explanation is to be found in Herder's role as a prophet of harmony of the soul and of culture; the analogue is that the highest goal of the mystic is harmony. Otherwise, the identification seems to be misleading. Herder's concern with the soul was particularly attractive to Grønbech, for whom nothing was more important than spiritual harmony, that is, a unity of urges, inclinations, and desires on the one hand, and thought and ideals upon the other. Grønbech had recognized the existence of a harmony in the Renaissance but the Renaissance was dead and gone and had had its severe limitations. A sort of new harmony that Herder envisaged was of "greater beauty, by virtue of his recognition of his own spirit, its experience within itself, and its sympathy with the experience of others."[20]

VI   William Blake

Some admirers and critics of Vilhelm Grønbech feel that his book on William Blake belongs among his most significant contributions. The subtitle, "Artist, Poet, Mystic," would seem to identify it as one of the volumes about mystics of India and Europe, but it was not included in that series, although issued in 1933, one year after

volumes II and III and one year before volume IV. In fact, Grønbech's foremost concern is not with the mystical aspect of Blake but
with Blake the artist and poet as a creater of myth. A great poet is
able to create myth and Grønbech viewed Blake as an unsurpassed
creative poet. He also viewed Blake as one of the most difficult of
poets. Indeed, he admits that not all of Blake is penetrable. It is
certain, however, that the reader of Blake needs a guide, at least at
first. Grønbech, whose interest in Blake went back to those early
years of the twentieth century when he was teaching English literature at the University of Copenhagen and whose competence was
derived from an intensive study of Blake's poetry over a long period
of time, would be such a guide for Danish readers. The particular
appeal of Blake for Grønbech is probably to be explained through
the fact that Blake is not an aesthetic poet. That is to say, his poems
are not lyrics in the usual sense of the word. The creation of new
images, and in particular mythical constructions, outweighs minor
aesthetic considerations of form. As has been observed elsewhere,
Grønbech was impatient with aesthetic criteria but was much given
to the identification of fundamental ideas.

As a critic of Blake, Grønbech was something of a pioneer. In
Denmark little attention had been paid to Blake previously, and
outside Denmark the critical penetration and analysis of Blake's
work was only getting under way. Grønbech was originally drawn to
Blake because of the intrinsic difficulty in understanding him. He
worked through Blake's writings thoroughly, recast much of what
Blake had written in his own words, interpreted the poet's images,
and made an effort to categorize many of his ideas. As is his wont,
Grønbech interprets Blake to a large extent through the use of
paraphrase. In this case the paraphrases are more nearly a poetic
rewriting of Blake in Danish; Grønbech's use of language in the
book on Blake has been affected by Blake's use of language. One
comes very near to Blake through Grønbech. Unlike other works by
Grønbech (except perhaps the collection of aphorisms by Friedrich
Schlegel published by the Danish Academy of Sciences in 1935) this
book uses a large amount of original text to bolster its arguments—
that is, quotations in the original English. Thus the reader often has
Blake at first hand. Because Grønbech is convinced of the unity that
exists between Blake's text and Blake's drawings, he also has repro-
duced a large number of Blake's drawings in the book so that the
reader is aided visually in the understanding of Blake's text,

whether in English or in Grønbech's Danish versions. Incidentally, one finds in the notes to the book on Blake several pages of Grønbech's direct translation from the prophetic books.

Grønbech respected William Blake because Blake perceived a different reality from most men and was able to explain if not to recreate it both in words and drawings, since he was both a poet and an artist. By Grønbech's definition, Blake was a mystic, since he lived in a world that transcended the everyday world of his fellow men, but he was also a prophet, since he could see more clearly than others, albeit in such a fashion that he appeared to be a strange visionary. He wrote in highly metaphorical language and employed images which, although symbolic, are scarcely symbols as the word is ordinarily used.

Grønbech's interpretation of Blake is a synthesis: the book is a reclassification and reordering of Blake's ideas and mythic creations. Unlike the literary historian, Grønbech is not concerned with Blake's biographical development or with the chronology of the works but rather with the philosophical unity of Blake's entire achievement. The most remarkable characteristic of Grønbech's book is indeed the fact that he is able to synthesize Blake, to put pieces together to create a whole, and to establish a system of concepts and images that, although arbitrary, is defensible and acceptable and gives the reader an understanding of the poet that he could scarcely have achieved for himself without the investment of unlimited time and energy. Because Grønbech's book is written in Danish, it has not caught the attention of Blake scholars outside Denmark and has never been critically compared with what might be called the standard interpretations of Blake published in English. It is safe to say, however, that Grønbech's book would stand comparison with English interpretations. Although it represents a personal view and is not an effort to take sides in the matter of English Blake scholarship, it may be assumed to have as much validity as other serious, comprehensive studies of Blake's work.

Grønbech was much taken by the drawings with which Blake accompanied his poetry. To Grønbech it seemed of greatest importance that art and knowledge found a unity in Blake. This unity he saw identifiable in Blake's drawings. Grønbech also applauded Blake's stress of Eros and the role of woman in a man's life. In this connection it is well to remember that Grønbech was an early champion of women's rights, as evidenced by his articles on that subject written in 1924. According to Grønbech, Eros led in Blake's view to a destruction of human fantasy and such a destruction was in itself sinful—a negation of an important aspect of existence.

Finally, Grønbech saw in Blake a prophet for whom the establishment of the kingdom of God was not merely a distant possibility but achievable in the same sense as Jesus envisaged it—according to Grønbech's interpretation in his *Jesus*, which appeared two years after the book on Blake.

CHAPTER 5

Confronting German Luminaries

I After Herder, Goethe

THERE is a complicated connection between Vilhelm Grønbech and three German titans from the end of the eighteenth and the beginning of the nineteenth century: Johann Gottfried Herder, Johann Wolfgang Goethe, and Friedrich Schlegel. His early active concern with them and the new world of thought of which they were important components dates back to *Religious Currents of the Nineteenth Century* in 1922. Here he takes a critical position vis-à-vis each of them and briefly characterizes their historical importance within the context of the general argument of that book. Subsequently he dealt with each of them in greater detail; first Herder, to whom a large section of the fourth volume of *Mystics* was devoted; then Friedrich Schlegel, many of whose aphorisms he turned into Danish; and finally Goethe, to whom he devoted a two volume study of the man and the poet. Of the three Germans, Herder was of the greatest importance to Grønbech, and Schlegel the least. The relationship with Herder was the most intimate; and for Herder Grønbech had the deepest sympathy and understanding. Herder was, moreover, the dominant figure in *Religious Currents*, for Herder was an early champion of the evolutionary concept and of the importance of popular culture. As has been mentioned before, Herder was in fact a model for Grønbech—and Grønbech has sometimes been called a twentieth-century Herder.

Grønbech's analysis of Herder's thought has been described in the chapter on mystics, and will not be repeated here save to say that in Herder Grønbech saw a kindred spirit who pointed the way to a harmony of the soul and therewith a harmony in society. For Grønbech this harmony, albeit possibly to be categorized as a mystic phenomenon, was the ultimate goal of human existence, a philosophic and religious ideal.

While it is not unexpected that Grønbech was attracted to the greatest of Germans or that he should write about him at length, it can scarcely be considered surprising that his attitude toward Goethe was so clearly ambivalent, for Goethe in no way embodied the ideal of a member of a body of believers. There are probably three reasons for Grønbech's interest in Goethe. First, Goethe must be considered the most notable single personality in Europe in modern times. Second, in his own life and works Goethe seemed to achieve an inner harmony. Third, Goethe possessed not a few characteristics in common with Grønbech himself: both were universal geniuses; both wrote authoritatively on many subjects; both were individualists convinced of their own authority.

Had Goethe not been a great poet, Grønbech would not have been attracted to him. Nevertheless, his first volume on Goethe, published in 1935, is a presentation of Goethe the man rather than Goethe the poet. Grønbech tries to explain who Goethe was and why he became the man he did. The volume may be characterized as an interpretive synthesis of all that Goethe wrote up to and during the Italian adventure. The style of volume I is easy and the book readable; Grønbech writes with enthusiasm and respect. It is noteworthy, however, that Grønbech's interest in Goethe becomes less personal and his attitude considerably more critical in volume II (1939).

Unlike his other books, *Goethe* is not characterized by a new and original interpretation. Grønbech's Goethe corresponds, rather, to the traditional Goethe of literary history. Grønbech makes no effort to give Goethe's biography a new twist but is satisfied rather to view his life through his work. This has been done so many times previously that there is a concensus regarding the younger Goethe. The role of the Italian journey in Goethe's life is also clearly a matter of record so that Grønbech's emphasis of the exploit is pleonastic. Grønbech also stresses Goethe's friendship with Schiller; and here, too, he is supporting a contention of established Goethe scholarship. More than most, Grønbech takes care to point out the union of the poet and the scientist in Goethe.

Grønbech begins his study with an interpretation of the young Goethe's lyrics and letters. He does this in order to penetrate

Goethe psychologically; he passes no aesthetic judgments on Goethe's language of imagery. He recognizes the importance that Frau von Stein had in Goethe's life and makes considerable use of Goethe's notes to her. Like many other writers on Goethe, he looks upon the journey to Italy as the turning point in Goethe's life; in fact, he draws a parallel between the trip to Italy for the mature Goethe and Goethe's meeting with Herder in the Strassburg in his youth. Goethe's searching mind appeals to Grønbech, and Grønbech therefore devotes attention to Goethe's scientific studies, notably to the concept of the *Urpflanze*.

Grønbech does not doubt Goethe's greatness as a master of human cognition and an imaginative writer, but there is necessarily a continuing reservation in his attitude toward Goethe since Goethe's goal in life was personal development and refinement. Rather, Grønbech is especially attentive to Goethe because Goethe sought a synthesis and sought harmony in nature, despite his lack of an understanding for the need of a community of believers.

Grønbech is less interested in the older Goethe; the greater length of the second volume of *Goethe* does not mean a corresponding increase in admiration for the German author on Grønbech's part. On the contrary, Grønbech uses the pejorative adjective "Hellenistic" about Goethe. Goethe's classicism is in Grønbech's eyes a result of Hellenistic philosophy. While "Hellenistic" is indeed an adjective that may be applied to our own time, Grønbech never applied it positively. For him it always carried a pejorative connotation. Some of the very traits that have recommended Goethe to many of his admirers in later decades Grønbech finds to be of doubtful value. In particular he is skeptical of the ideal of personal development—"die persönliche Bildung." Personal development and Goethe's native genius tended to make Goethe thoughtless of persons who were uninteresting to him and from whom he could derive no benefit.

Some of Grønbech's judgments of several of Goethe's major works are eccentric. Thus he rejects *Die Wahlverwandtschaften (Elective Affinities)* as imaginative literature despoiled by pseudoscientific demonstration and as unreal and sentimental. He would explain the novel as a reflex of Goethe's relationship with Marianne von Willemer. Grønbech was, however, kindly disposed to *Dichtung und Wahrheit (Poetry and Truth)*, which he considered one of Goethe's masterpieces, perhaps because it is more an autobiography than it is a novel. *Faust* Grønbech looked upon as the history of Goethe's own soul and a work that devolves into aestheticism in its use of Christian symbols. Grønbech believed that any closer interpretation of *Faust* necessitates an intimate knowledge of Goethe's life in Weimar—an attitude that was usually overlooked in Goethe scholarship in the early years of the twentieth century. Grønbech nevertheless attempts an interpretation of *Faust*, which he—like most readers— finds a difficult work that cannot be understood literally. The symbolism he considers inaccessible presumably because there are so many allusions to life in Weimar that the drama is incomprehensible without some kind of biographical commentary. Although Grønbech's opinions seem highly subjective, they can serve as a point of origin for further discussion. German Goethe scholarship has taken a standoffish attitude toward Grønbech's discussion of *Faust* in part because it is subjective, in part because it is pragmatic, in part because it makes no effort at aesthetic analysis.

Goethe was both important *per se* and because he was a corporeal symbol of the new time. Goethe's problem was the problem of the time, and specifically the problem of the relation between reality and actuality. Goethe's neoclassicism was the neoclassicism of the late eighteenth century. Goethe's Greek was an eighteenth-century Greek, but he spoke a modern secular language that distinguished his explanations and formulations from the argot of traditional philosophy. Goethe was a philosopher and as a philosopher he was ever more an observer than a theorist. One is reminded of the beginning of the biography of Goethe by the German scholar Karl Viëtor, who quotes Goethe to the effect that, "When he turned eighteen, Germany had just turned eighteen."[1] The maturing of Goethe meant also the maturing of German literature and German thought—and there was indeed an interplay of forces. Goethe was molded in part by the politically fragmented Germany in which he lived; but he also molded that Germany that was becoming unified culturally.

Grønbech emphasizes that Goethe's knowledge of both Greek and English literature, which in retrospect seem to have been important determinants for the European eighteenth century, was narrow and limited; but for Goethe this knowledge sufficed and he used it repeatedly and audaciously. He did not lack confidence in his own interpretations; nor did he wince because of lacunae in his factual knowledge.

Grønbech characterizes Goethe as a creative artist who would exploit a "higher nature." To be sure, "nature" provided for Goethe the basis for cognition, but the experiencing of nature and of reality remained problematic. "What the world needs," Grønbech lets Goethe say, "is a thoroughgoing reform of experience itself comparable to philosophical self-reflection."[2] The allusion here is, of course, to Kant. If art is to progress, in Goethe's opinion, there is required a critique of the senses comparable to Kant's critique of reason. Goethe is nevertheless not really a friend of reality, and not a realist in the modern sense of the word. The idea, states Grønbech, not the acceptance of actuality, was Goethe's reality. As an example of Goethe's relationship to actuality, Grønbech uses Goethe's foremost neoclassical achievement, the play *Iphigenie in Aulis*. Grønbech contrasts Goethe's play with Euripides' on the same subject: "Everything that could disturb the pure, humane idea, all the unfitting passions which could effect a tragic clash between persons, are gone as with the wind."[3]

Goethe, then, is no revolutionary, even though he personifies modern times. He accepted the societal hierarchy into which he was born. He was satisfied to spend most of his life within the narrow confines that Weimar—tiny capital of a tiny dukedom—set. He was a de facto rational Protestant, despite his nominal rejection of organized Christianity. His liaison with Christiane was bold, but it was ultimately legalized by the church. Like Grønbech himself, Goethe was critical of a multitude of institutions, but he did not participate in any practical effort to effect radical changes. The changes that could evolve from a social evolution rather than revolution, however, were acceptable and desirable. Evolutionary change was in concord with the principle of *Steigerung*—progression—which was essential in Goethe's own philosophy of life and interpretation of the world.

Volume II contains a large amount of Goethe either in quotations or paraphrase. A parallel can be drawn between this volume and the work on Friedrich Schlegel which Grønbech had published the same year that volume I of *Goethe* had appeared. The same question that was asked of the Schlegel book can then be asked: Was it worth Grønbech's time and energy to transpose such a large amount of Goethe's text into Danish, when nearly every educated Dane was in a position to read Goethe in the original German? By an excision of paraphrases, if not also of direct quotation in German, Grønbech might have produced a much smaller—and presumably more forceful—work, which would constitute his own interpretation of the mature and older Goethe. In fact, there is little interpretation of the poetry that Grønbech quotes: he is apparently trying to let the poetry speak for itself. The method is not very effective, since Grønbech consistently eschews aesthetic criticism and heeds only the narrative and ethical content of poetry.

That Grønbech concerned himself with Goethe is significant in Danish intellectual history, but the fact is of relatively little intrinsic importance, since Grønbech's *Goethe* lacks a good deal of the fire and brilliance that many of his other books possess. For Grønbech, Goethe's works were almost exclusively autobiographical documents. There is no attempt made to separate the persona of the author from the author himself, nor is there any other assumption than the tacit one that all of Goethe's works are indeed, to use Goethe's own phrase, parts of a great confession. Goethe as presented in volume I of Grønbech's study is an agreeable figure, a human being, and not yet the metaphysical creation that predominates in volume II. In his youth, and increasingly during his stay in Italy in his thirties, Goethe approached an harmonious existence. In volume II Goethe is an introspective, self-satisfied, saturnine titan, who was concerned with aesthetic values rather than public welfare. Since Grønbech never was sympathetic to aestheticism, Goethe's turn to the aesthetic and away from the ethical—to use Kierke-gaardian terminology—was distasteful to Grønbech. He could not fully accept the mature Goethe as both a monumental and admirable figure.

In volume II of his *Goethe* Grønbech gives a succinct view of the eighteenth century that may be quoted in part here:

. . . a time of reassessment, the beginning of the decline of aristocratic culture and aristocratic religion. The practical reassessment which developed in the hundred years following, was still only making noises in the background; the revolution in France was a volcanic eruption which was of temporary importance in revealing what was fermenting underground. In all areas one could note the threat of the future evoking vague panic among the spiritual aristocrats; it was as if they felt the ground giving way beneath them. The philosophers continued to construct the universe out of traditional concepts, but in ambush behind their systems was the doubt that the concepts possessed any reality. Criticism was the order of the day, that is to say, the relationship between thought and reality. Is there something real behind our concepts or are they but a figment of our imagination? This question arose, consciously or unconsciously. Is everything we live by only a poetic construction which we have erected in order to achieve some cohesion in our perceptions? Is the world which we have built up during a thousand years, with its division of spirit and material, nothing but a fata morgana?[4]

Grønbech could praise both Goethe and Herder before him because each had achieved harmony. Herder had pointed to the understanding of various cultures; Goethe also to a salvation through art. The so-called German Romantics, Friedrich Schlegel and Novalis in particular, had wider horizons. Grønbech calls them a "generation unafraid." Young men have revolution in the blood and "their experience forces them to sympathize with all the shapes which the spirit has assumed in history, and they see the classical religions as well as Christianity as necessary expressions of a life of the soul."[5] For this attitude Grønbech has complete understanding and he looked upon that younger generation as containing forerunners of the kind of history of religion that he himself represented. Yet this history of religion equated religion with mythology, as one must conclude from an examination of the new thinkers around 1800, particularly Friedrich Schlegel and Friedrich Schleiermacher, whom Grønbech looked upon as an inspiration to the theologians of the first half of the century. For Grønbech myth was not something aberrant but the key that unlocked the door leading to harmony, whether through an analytical understanding of the past or a constructive effort to create a better future.

II   Friedrich Schlegel

That Grønbech turned his attention to the German writers and thinkers Goethe and Herder as central figures in the history of European culture and thought may be considered unavoidable, especially in view of the parallelism that may be recognized between Grønbech in his time and the two German titans in theirs, but that he could produce a lengthy book on the stormy young critic Friedrich Schlegel, whose name is regularly associated with that uncertain label "German Romanticism," is unexpected and is indicative of considerable perspicacity and foresight. Schlegel's significance has really only been recognized since World War II, after the oversimplified categorization with which he earlier tended to be pushed to one side by literary historians was overcome. There is no doubt that Schlegel was himself at fault in engendering a misleading picture of himself, first as the author of the unfinished novel *Lucinde* (which was supposed to cause readers to raise an eyebrow because of its sensuousness) and in particular because of the hymn to idleness that the novel contained and that was assumed to be representative of Schlegel's own convictions and personality. It is easy enough today to perceive the importance of a writer possessed of Schlegel's fertile mind and facile pen whose works, now being collected for the first time, embrace many volumes, but Grønbech saw what others did not see among his contemporaries. He pleaded Schlegel's cause at length with an emphasis upon Schlegel's aphorisms which are interpreted paraphrastically. His text without notes comprises 425 printed pages, 150 of them Danish versions of the aphorisms. Grønbech seems to have been a voice in the wilderness, for his book evoked no response. There were two reasons for the lack of interest: first, as it was written in Danish, the work could not expect to be read by many scholars outside Denmark; second, it was issued as a volume of the historical-philological reports of the Danish Academy of Sciences—and had therefore no chance to reach a larger public or even to attract the attention of the commercially oriented press. Of all Grønbech's works, *Friedrich Schlegel i årene 1791–1808* (1935) has remained the least known, buried in a series where even scholars who might benefit from it could scarcely be expected to find it.[6] Today we may feel it a great pity that Grønbech expended so much time and effort to produce his book on Friedrich Schlegel, since it was overlooked in its own time and, although its theses are by no means superseded today, cannot be expected to have an impact upon the scholarship that has seen the rise of a new "Schlegel philology" which in many ways has come to reiterate views expressed by Grønbech over forty years ago. Further, that so much material by Schlegel which has been published in the interim was not available to Grønbech is also to the detriment of Grønbech's study.

The convictions that inform *Friedrich Schlegel* are basically a continuation of the argument that Grønbech had initiated in the *Religious Currents;* the reader will recall that a chapter of that earlier work was devoted to Friedrich Schlegel as a successor to Goethe and Schiller and a leading member of the new current of literature that came to the fore in Germany around 1800. In Grønbech's eyes, the young Friedrich Schlegel was a radical representative of the new

time which at the end of the eighteenth century finally made a break
with the metaphysical world of the Middle Ages and the Reformation that held sway until the final victory of rationalism and enlightenment, "when men found it necessary to prove the existence
of God" and therewith brought about the demise of their God
around 1770. We must remember, however, that Friedrich
Schlegel was also an apostate. A champion of the new religious
currents at the very beginning of the nineteenth century, he was
soon to fall back into the arms of the church of Rome. Thus he was
no longer interesting to Grønbech after 1808, that is, after his conversion. That Friedrich Schlegel had not a little in common with
Johann Gottfried Herder was an idea which Grønbech had also
expressed in 1922 in *Religious Currents*. After having devoted an
essay to Herder in volume IV of *Mystics in India and Europe,*
Grønbech touched on this relationship again in the volume on
Schlegel in 1935. The relationship seems fairly tenuous; nevertheless, in the case of Friedrich Schlegel and in that of Herder, Grønbech saw not only two figures from the past with whom he was
willing to identify himself but two figures who have constantly
grown in importance in cultural history as it has been developed
during the last forty years. Friedrich Schlegel was moreover something of a bridge between Herder and Goethe for Grønbech, who
saw a logical sequence in the development of ideas from the older
Herder to the younger Schlegel with Goethe the intermediate—
mediating—and monumental figure. The interrelationship of these
persons for Grønbech is emphasized by the fact that the essay on
Herder appeared in 1934 and the first volume of Goethe as well as
the work on Friedrich Schlegel in the next year, 1935. The book
devoted to Schlegel is an amalgam rather than a synthesis of paraphrase and interpretation.

Grønbech was able to extend to Friedrich Schlegel the label of
mystic because Schlegel experienced unity of existence—a new reality of modern time. Grønbech loses interest in Schlegel after the
conversion to Roman Catholicism, however, since he feels that
Schlegel then gave up his struggle for the acquisition of the new
reality that was so important in the new literature around the turn of
the century. The aphoristic, the fragmentary, the incomplete
work—these were indeed characteristic of the new literature and of
Friedrich Schlegel, but they are not to be considered as negative

characteristics but, rather, essays into a new reality, bricks as it were for the new metaphysical structure of modern time.

As he was wont to do, Grønbech began by examining important concepts or, more precisely, important words in Friedrich Schlegel's writing, but he immediately made the point that with his subject there was a semantic problem of primary importance. Schlegel might use the same words as Goethe or Herder, but these words had a different meaning for him than they did for the pillars of German classicism. "All too often," Grønbech writes on the first page of the book on Schlegel, "psychology is treated as if it were spiritual mathematics; an equal sign is placed between the glosses common to the language of geniuses and the unknown is figured out as if it were an equation . . . ,"[7] whereas in reality the differences in usage often are very great. "Only when one examines the words from within, do they reveal themselves,"[8] Grønbech comments— and this remark is a summation of what might be identified as Grønbech's method in those of his works that endeavour to ascertain the basic assumptions of a culture or a religion or a philosophy. With respect to Schlegel, Grønbech begins by mentioning the term "harmony." Harmony was basic to the German classics; it was also basic to Friedrich Schlegel—but the respective concepts of harmony were not really compatible. "For Goethe and Herder," writes Grønbech, "everything was contained in the word evolution; for Schlegel, life's word was revolution."[9] It is understandable then, that there could be no reconciliation between Herder and Goethe on the one hand and the young Friedrich Schlegel on the other. Goethe and Herder, Grønbech explains, are free of catastrophe and crisis, whereas Friedrich Schlegel seems to incorporate irreconcilable contradictions.

At this Grønbech launches into a discussion of the two concepts of activity and idleness that are important to Schlegel and would seem to be opposites. Opposites they may be, but Grønbech makes clear their interdependence and how, for Schlegel, creativity could be born of their interplay. Grønbech exemplifies his point by the mystery of love: at the very juncture where man and woman abandon themselves to the forces of nature and themselves cease conscious activity toward any goal, the moment of creation is achieved. Passivity, says Grønbech, thus becomes the ultimate activity. And this Schlegel realized.

Grønbech thereupon discusses the meaning of enthusiasm and love for Schlegel; and the terms are seen to be interrelated. For Schlegel enthusiasm is not the emotionalism of Goethe's *Werther* or the pervasive sentimentalism of late eighteenth-century literature. Enthusiasm and love are for Schlegel passion rather than emotion; moreover, they suggest the longing for the infinite that transcends the limitations that man hitherto has felt. The corollary of this principle—a corollary which, to be sure, Grønbech himself does not formulate—is that once the borders of the known can be transcended and the traditional limitations of man's knowledge can be dismissed, the possibilities for new scientific discovery also became limitless: the stage is set for the dominance of new scientific theories in the nineteenth century. This is, of course, an idea that lay at the base of Grønbech's discussion of the *Religious Currents of the Nineteenth Century* in 1922.

The biographical section that follows is less lucid than Grønbech's discussion of key concepts in Schlegel. Grønbech contrasts Schlegel's concept of the past with that of Goethe and Schiller and sets up Schlegel as a counterpart to Schiller as an aesthetic philosopher. The diffuse argument is not convincing, but it is soon replaced by the 150 pages devoted to Danish versions of Schlegel's aphorisms. They are probably as stimulating in Grønbech's paraphrases as in Schlegel's German but one wonders for whom Grønbech undertook the task. Any Danish scholar who might read publications of the Academy of Science could also read German. He might find Grønbech's categorization of the aphorisms of some interest, but few if any readers of German could be expected to devote the time needed to read so many of the aphorisms in Danish, although the Danish versions are not simply translations, to be sure. Moreover, by their very nature they do not lend themselves to syntheses, although Grønbech would admit Schlegel's own thesis that the fragments, for all their chaotic confusion, "comprise a whole." Grønbech seems closer to the mark when he calls the aphorisms glimpses of a living soul. "The literary unity," he writes, "consists in the glimpses of crossing flashes of lightning suddenly illuminating part of a human soul," but this observation seems to be no more than a self-serving metaphor.[10]

CHAPTER 6

Understanding Early Christianity

I Jesus

IN *The Culture of the Teutons* Grønbech had addressed himself to
the matter of a cohesive Germanic culture and a community of
Scandinavian believers in the Middle Ages, both because the subject of Germanic antiquity is intrinsically interesting and because it
represents the indigenous Scandinavian past. In the 1920s and early
1930s he had spoken to a number of more recent phenomena that,
to a greater or lesser extent, possess dynamism in the twentieth
century: the spiritual convolutions that Western civilization has experienced since the end of the eighteenth century, with particular
reference to the rise of new scientific thought in the nineteenth
century, as well as to contemporary problems as variegated as liter-
acy and the labor movement. Grønbech demonstrated a desire to
perceive and identify currents and forces that willy-nilly had molded
and were molding our own society. Always attracted to the positive
quality of a strong religious conviction and to the force of myth,
Grønbech had also delved into individual aspects of religious
phenomena currently being expressed both in more traditional ways
and through the medium of imaginative literature.

Given these preoccupations and predilections, Grønbech could
not be expected to disregard the greatest single religious and cultural force in the history of Western civilization: Christianity. Nor
could he be expected to produce a history of Christianity—for that
would smack too much of pragmatism. Early Christianity, representing a community of believers, and early Christianity in its religious, philosophical, and ethical assumptions, however, could not
fail to attract Grønbech's strong interest and to engage his analytical
mind. Between 1935 and 1941 three volumes were published devoted to the subject: *Jesus*, *Paulus*, and *Kristus*. Between the first

81

two, however, Grønbech wrote a two-volume study of Hellenism—which is a necessary complement of the trilogy on Christianity.

In *Jesus* (1935) Grønbech attempted an interpretation solely on
the basis of the words of the Saviour as preserved in the Gospels of
Matthew, Mark, and Luke. While he was skeptical about descrip-
tive material in the New Testament, he felt that the words of Jesus
had indeed been preserved literally in the first three Gospels, if
only because of the great respect in which the Master was held by
His disciples. The book was nevertheless a personal interpretation
and generated considerable anguish in some critics upon publication. It called forth some angry words by reviewers who were unwilling to accept what they considered to be an unhistorical and
demythologized Jesus in Grønbech's book. Like all of Grønbech's
other books, *Jesus* was written with great sympathy for the subject,
although Grønbech's may be called a radical evaluation, in particular because he did not address himself to the question of the divinity
of Jesus; the subtitle of the book was "Son of Man." *Jesus* has
nevertheless been Grønbech's most widely read work. It has been
the most frequently reissued of all his books and since 1964 has been
available in an inexpensive paperback edition. The book has found
appreciative readers for four decades.

It is easy to see why Grønbech's book on Jesus evoked more
comment than his other works. Not only is the subject *per se* one of
greater appeal in the Christian world and not only is Grønbech's
interpretation original and challenging—*Jesus* is written in a simpler
and more forthright style than are most of Grønbech's previous
books. One may look upon it as a turning point in his production and
as the first of the more popular books that won him a wider audience
in the 1940s and early 1950s. The presentation of material in *Jesus* is
also less verbose than in the earlier works. Since the traditional
words of Jesus preserved in the New Testament are relatively simple and striking, Grønbech—adapting himself as ever to his subject
as he understood it—now wrote in a simpler and more striking
fashion.

More than in his other works, Grønbech attempts in *Jesus* to jolt
his reader. He bandies generalities that are bound to startle the
traditional Christian believer. Although not the intent of the book,
the effect is akin to that of a popular evangelical sermon. Grønbech
has tried to divorce the words of Jesus from their antiquated

background and to dissolve the historical patina that they have acquired in traditional translation. He presents Jesus as something of a misfit by describing Him from the standpoint of the Jewish society, for which Jesus represented an imminent danger. Grønbech wanted to make clear what was novel and what was unexpected in Jesus' vocabulary. He stresses many of the words that must have grated on the ears of contemporary Jews—although we moderns have heard these words so many times that they no longer possess any special force and, because of their association with Jesus, have acquired acceptability and respectability, whereas in Jesus' own time they could not have been considered acceptable nor were they meant to be casually acceptable when spoken. Grønbech makes the point that many of Jesus' statements and especially His metaphors were not self-evident when they first were enunciated. Grønbech suggests that all the metaphors originally meant more than they superficially seem to mean now.

In *Jesus* Vilhelm Grønbech had the obvious intent of making the Messiah appear real, actual, and alive, for his is a modern psychological depiction. While he assumes the existence of concepts two thousand years ago to be different from those which obtain in the present day, he does not assume that the human mind then differed from the human mind now. Because he is familiar with the canonical texts of the New Testament, he has self-assurance and conviction in his rendition of the canonical words of Jesus. He permits himself liberties in his paraphrases, but he is not being arbitrary or demagogic after the manner of an hortatory cleric. On the one hand his interpretation of Jesus is a personal one, but on the other it is a sincere effort to penetrate to the inner meaning of preserved traditions and in particular of the diction of the Master.

Jesus is not, but might have been, a sectarian interpretation of the New Testament. In another age Vilhelm Grønbech might have come to be looked upon as a religious leader or as the founder of some protesting sect. That was out of the question, however, for Grønbech was no friend of modern, managerially organized religion. His skepticism toward organized religion and formal religious services is evident, for example, where he mentions "an edifying sermon of the same kind one can hear today if one takes the trouble of going into a church."[1] He was never orthodox and probably never kindly disposed to orthodox theologians. It is not surprising, therefore, that the most febrile attacks upon *Jesus* came from the camp of

conservative theologians who branded Grønbech's book as dangerous and misleading. *Jesus* was nevertheless kindly received by many
Danish clergymen who understood Grønbech's motivation in writing such an interpretation and who appreciated the imaginative and
poetic quality of his language. A sympathetic reviewer of the
Swedish translation of *Jesus* (1936) wrote, "The picture of Jesus
which one obtains from Grønbech is in brief that He is alive, and if
one should taste the 'salt in Jesus' speech' that speech had to be
translated to everyday language."[2] The reviewer expressed the hope
that Grønbech might undertake to rewrite the entire New Testament after the same fashion.

Grønbech makes much of Jesus' being a revolutionary in his own
time and of the cleft between the attitudes of Jesus on the one hand
and the mores of contemporary Jewish society on the other. He
endeavors to show us both sides of the coin, to present the Jesus
who is a blasphemer and also to present the Jesus who dissipates the
air of sanctimony that envelops pharisees and hypocrites. Grønbech
would make his reader understand how difficult it must have been
for those who heard Jesus, including His own apostles, to grasp the
simplicity and at the same time the realism of His message, to
understand clearly the intent of His didactic parables and His dis-
dain of ritual when ritual contradicted reason.

The elevated quality of Biblical language to which we are accustomed in translations of the sacred books, Grønbech counteracts in
the modern, simple, and sometimes even flippant language that he
employs in order to achieve an air of actuality and to make the
reader realize that what Jesus said is applicable in daily life and is
not mere poetic speech meant to resound only from the walls of a
church. The rhythmical nature and rhetorical quality of Grønbech's
own language serves to counterbalance the dignified and archaic
language of most Bible translation. Parallel, repetition, hyperbole,
and alliteration are frequently employed by Grønbech to create
lively, forceful, and distinct impressions. Such devices differentiate
his presentation of Jesus, linguistically modern as it may be, from
mere pedestrian and careless everyday speech. Here and there he
does employ a Biblical word or phrase, however, in order to inject a
more serious, elevated note into his narrative and to awaken associations in the soul of the reader.

Since Jesus is for Grønbech the Son of Man and not an an-
thropomorphic God, Grønbech is not afraid to imply weaknesses in

the methods that Jesus employed and in some of the decisions He made. Grønbech points out that there are contradictions in Jesus' prophecy and ambiguities in some of His actions. Time and again Grønbech speaks from the standpoint of a contemporary of Jesus who is a serious and reasonable observer and who nevertheless must shake his head from lack of comprehension of something Jesus said or did.

It is a notable characteristic of *Jesus* that Grønbech's narrative and interpretation conclude with the Last Supper. There is no attempt to describe the crucifixion and no mention of events thereafter. It almost had to be thus in any work that attempted solely to draw upon the words of Jesus as source material.

Grønbech looked upon Jesus as an agitator in the world of the spirit. Grønbech felt that the church and the legend of Jesus grew concomitantly and nourished one another as something apart from the historical Jesus or the Jesus of the Gospels. Jesus, according to Grønbech, was trying to teach people how to live and how to create the kingdom of God on earth. This is what made Jesus attractive in Grønbech's eyes, and this is why Grønbech insists upon identifying Him as the Son of Man.

Some evidence would seem to imply that Grønbech's own relationship to the traditional Christian religion was either ambivalent or objective to the point of agnosticism. In writing about various persuasions he regularly identified himself with them in a sympathetic fashion, so that one could not perceive his own bias. He assiduously avoided making statements about himself that could be construed as an admission of faith or adherence—in particular to the established Danish Lutheran Church. He felt it to be an unwarranted intrusion when, out of curiosity, someone asked him about his own religious belief or whether he accepted a personal God. There is nevertheless indisputable evidence of his own predilection for Christianity, or at least his admiration for the teachings of Jesus. Superficially, this characteristic is demonstrable by pointing to his not infrequent use of the parables of Jesus, even when one might have considered the subject with which he dealt to be outside a Christian context. More striking, however, is the inclusion of one poem from his first collection of verse, *Morituri* (1903), in the later collection of verse, *Solen har mange veje* (1941). In the earlier volume, the poem in question gave the collection its pessimistic title: "Ave, imperator, morituri." In the later volume, the poem was entitled

"Menneskesønnen"—"The Son of Man"—the last word of the original poem. One immediately senses a continuity of thought spanning four decades and at the same time the association with Grønbech's book on Jesus, which bore the subtitle "The Son of Man."

Thus, Grønbech was and remained an admirer of the historical Jesus, whether he accepted the divinity of the Saviour or not.

From Grønbech's point of view, early Christianity offered a new myth and did indeed function as a new myth, despite the dissension within the early church which he describes in the book *Kristus*. The myth disintegrated in the eighteenth century with the victory of rationalism, however, as he so poignantly depicted in *Religious Currents of the Nineteenth Century*. This did not mean that Christianity was wrong—or right, for that matter—but rather that men had asked new questions and lost their faith. Whatever might happen to organized religion, the debilitated and disintegrated Christian church nevertheless preserved a remnant of the spiritual communality of earlier times. If medieval Christianity could not be resuscitated, it could nevertheless provide a model of a functioning myth and union of the faithful. Moreover, the words of Jesus could not be eradicated.

II *Hellenism*

A companion volume to *Jesus*, dealing with Paul, was originally scheduled for publication soon after *Jesus* had appeared in 1935. We know that Grønbech was working on his book about Paul in 1936. Nevertheless, the completed book did not appear until four years later, in the autumn of 1940. The unusual time lag in Grønbech's late—and most productive—years required explanation. Grønbech's interest in Paul had had much meaning for him, for it led him on to a study of the background before which Paul appeared, the so-called Hellenistic culture of Greece and more particularly Rome at the beginning of the Christian era. Grønbech's intent was originally simply to sketch the outlines of Hellenistic culture as an introduction to the study of Paul, but as he familiarized himself with that culture, he was moved to describe it critically and in greater detail. In an independent work, issued in two volumes as *Hellenismen* in 1940 (with 1939 on the title page), Grønbech's approach to Hellenistic culture can in a limited fashion be compared with his approach to Old Germanic culture in *The Culture of the Teutons*. His concern is in determining the most important concepts that informed Hellenism and in identifying and describing the literary monuments produced in Rome under the impact of classical Greek culture, above all the work of Virgil. Grønbech dealt also with Plutarch, Diogenes Laertios, and many other writers.

Hellenism is a relatively new concept in the history of culture and religion; for Grønbech it was conveniently flexible and expansive. For him it embraced roughly the years 300 B.C. to 300 A.D. As in the case of *The Culture of the Teutons,* one can therefore question the overall temporal validity of Grønbech's observations. The geographical area under consideration is somewhat more clearly bounded in the book on Hellenism than in the earlier study, but the peculiarities of Hellenistic culture that Grønbech so incisively identifies can scarcely have obtained in an unchanging constellation for several hundred years. There is, then, an artificiality about Grønbech's metaphysical construct of Hellenism.

The work on Hellenism is a grand synthesis. There is no attempt at chronological-historical delineation. The underlying question remains, How much cultural unity actually existed in the relatively long period with which Grønbech was dealing. Moreover, many generalizations are found in the book on Hellenism that seem to have no direct connection with the subject. They are explicable only when viewed from the standpoint that our times presents a parallel to Hellenism and that Grønbech was intent upon making his readers aware of the parallel for didactic reasons. By laying the foibles of Hellenistic Rome bare, he was indirectly criticizing that comparable world in which he himself lived. Time and again in the work on Hellenism one finds generalizations that indicate that Grønbech is not speaking to his historical subject but passing a judgment on the present as well as the past. Thus in the chapter on "The Values of Life," one could apply sentence after sentence to the culture and civilization of the twentieth century. Consider, for example, the remark that "nature, the given basis for human life in reality, contains all the conditions to be a human being, but one becomes a human being only by working out and perfecting natural aptitudes. Nature does not acquire its proper appearance before it takes shape—and that happens through art."[3]

One must always bear in mind that Grønbech was first a student of language and second an historian of religion. Although he may be dealing with Roman literary works, he is not involved in a critical evaluation of those works from an aesthetic point of view. Or rather, when he attempts a critical evaluation of the poetry, he applies principles that were accepted in the Hellenistic era. As is his wont, Grønbech devotes considerable space to a retelling of various works—notably Virgil's *Aeneid*—about which he is writing. The retelling is necessarily also interpretive, however. In his lengthy résumé of the *Aeneid*, Grønbech is, as is so frequently the case, an ironic observer, so that the *Aeneid* acquires a bourgeois caste. Grønbech contrasts Virgil with Homer, to Virgil's disadvantage: Homer is realistic and straightforward, where Virgil is sentimental and affected.

Jesus had appealed to a very wide audience and was readily accessible to any interested reader in a Christian society; *Hellenismen* made considerably more demands upon the reader. Indeed, it is nearly impossible to follow Grønbech's argument in volume I if one does not have some familiarity with Epictetus, Marcus Aurelius, and Virgil. Despite its requiring prerequisites for understanding its historicity, the book is essentially an endeavor to describe a society that can be considered comparable to modern European society—with similar weaknesses and similar strengths. Time and again, Grønbech points out parallels that may be drawn between the world Virgil describes and our own times, even to the extent of humorously using anachronisms to make his point. Grønbech believes that, then as now, the poet had taken over the function of the priest; some of his activities were sacred. The poet spoke on behalf of the people to which he belonged, and often gave men what they were seeking. One is reminded of the role of the book in modern society as Grønbech explained it in the beginning of his essay "On Reading" (1922).

Grønbech is especially interested in the revaluation of ethical principles that occurred in Hellenistic time—once again a phenomenon that can be looked upon as a parallel to the social unrest of the twentieth century. Like our own culture, Hellenism suffered from unsatisfied longing, to a degree because there was more reflection upon life than the living of life. Today's reader is surprised to find such champions of traditional ethical values as Cicero and Seneca critically and even depreciatively discussed, whereas Grønbech seems to be sympathetically inclined to Epicurus and to the agnostics.

In *Hellenism* not the hero but the bourgeois dominates, and Grønbech devotes a chapter of his work to the bourgeois. Grønbech writes not only with sympathy but with some pity about the citizen of the Hellenistic world and his "ingrown optimism in the midst of the universe that has no meaning."[4] The world has no meaning in part because the Hellenistic god or gods are dead in the same sense that the old God of the Christian era is dead, as Grønbech had enunciated at the beginning of *Religious Currents*.

In an era when the gods are dead, it is understandable that salvation is to be sought through philosophy or through agnosticism. Grønbech's sympathetic treatment of certain philosophers and of the agnostics is a consequence, particularly because Grønbech recognizes that the agnostics wanted to keep man from starting down some path that was falsely labeled as the way to salvation. The Roman philosophers had to acquiesce to a religious state of affairs where the gods, in whom men no longer believed, nevertheless were the subject of ritual and celebration. The symbolism of the gods lived on although the gods themselves did not, and it was a function of the thinkers of the time to produce a satisfactory apology for this state of affairs.

Striking is the fact that the organization of Roman society, or perhaps, more accurately, of the Roman state, was seen to be a mirroring of the order in the natural world. The thinkers representative of this state, and in particular Cicero, must therefore be considered to be religious men. This is a viewpoint that presumably can be called original with Grønbech.

For all his reservations, skepticism, and irony, Grønbech does not view Hellenism as static. On the contrary, he identifies it as a period of change and revaluation, particularly in the realm of morality. Hellenistic man was adrift because he had lost the direct association with reality that had existed in earlier times. As a consequence, the Hellenistic writer becomes, in Grønbech's terms, a "pathetic artist" who no longer speaks directly from experience, who emphasizes the aesthetic quality of language, and whose work exudes learning.

In parts of the book on Hellenism, Grønbech quotes and paraphrases so extensively that it is difficult to identify and follow the argument he himself would make.[5] In contrast to the overall tendency toward gregariousness in paraphrase, Grønbech's treatment of the mystery religions—which comprises one of the most interesting aspects of Hellenistic culture—is brief, although not because Grønbech is unfamiliar with the source material (relatively speaking, he cites it extensively). The reason that the mystery religions

received short shrift probably is to be explained by Grønbech's plan
to write a third volume on Hellenism. This volume was never completed, although that part of it which dealt with Philo existed as a
fragment at Grønbech's death in 1948 and was subsequently edited
by Povl Johannes Jensen and published separately (1949).

Nor does Grønbech discuss such distinctive and important
phenomena as Judaism or early Christianity in the book on Hellenism. Since Hellenism was essentially meant as an introduction to
his work on Paul, this is less surprising. Grønbech had, however,
originally intended to write on Judaism, but his friend Johannes
Pedersen had published *Israel* (1920–34), which in concept and
execution was so similar to Grønbech's *The Culture of the
Teutons*—although it represented independent scholarship and
owed at most a debt to impulses that Pedersen had received from
conversations with Grønbech—that Grønbech felt that the need for
him to undertake a separate assessment and interpretation of
Judaism was not so pressing and could be postponed. Early Christianity was, however, subsequently the subject of Grønbech's *Kristus* in 1941.

The section on "moralists" in the study of Hellenism is less ironic
and more appreciative than the retelling of Virgil's *Aeneid*. Grønbech is skeptical of Hellenism because of its overwhelming concern
regarding morality. He writes humorously that "in Hellenism every
day is wash day"[6] and that the goal of a human being is to become a
beautiful soul. The Hellenistic man is not a person who acts but a
person who suffers, for all activity is for him directed inward.[7] Despite a characteristic dislike of the finger wagging that is associated
with a moralistic thinker, Grønbech is actually presenting a multitude of values that Western society has accepted for two millennia,
although man rarely has fulfilled the stoic and ascetic ideal of the
Greek and Roman moralists. Grønbech creates very much of a
synthesis of writers like Seneca and Marcus Aurelius, Epictetus,
and Plutarch. Without reference to his notes, one cannot be sure
which of the moralists he is quoting at any given moment or with
whose ideas one is confronted. Grønbech speaks with considerable
irony about the stoic philosophers. While he must be presumed to
have shared many of the same ideas that are expressed by Marcus
Aurelius, Epictetus, and Seneca in their works, Grønbech is ever
skeptical of asceticism. Grønbech discovers the perfect definition of

the world of Hellenism in Seneca: God has put all that is good within us and all that is inconsequential outside us.[8]

Throughout his presentation, Grønbech's position vis-à-vis Hellenism is ambivalent. On the one hand, the Hellenistic world is not an ideal that one should try to reachieve. On the other, it is a world comparable to our own in which there are voices to which one should listen. The analytical thinkers of the Hellenistic era provide criticism and remedies that have validity for the twentieth century as well as for the time they were conceived. The understanding of life in late classical Greece and Rome is similar to a Western understanding of life today. Although Grønbech does not take the trouble specifically to point this out, the parallelism is not accidental since Western civilization is to a large extent derivative from Hellenistic culture; it is indeed an extension of Hellenism, for the ultimate cultural affiliation of the nations of the West is with Greece and Rome.

Grønbech found the poetry of Hellenism to be pathetic and its import to lie precisely in its aesthetic quality. The Hellenistic poet is no longer speaking for a people and reformulating its myths, legends, and traditions but is speaking of his own experiences, his own pathos. "For the average person there is something amazing about Hellenistic poetry: that grown men can accept as their life's work to transfer their erotic difficulties into verse." But, says Grønbech, the average person's amazement arises because he does not understand the seriousness of life. The verses do not deal simply with a relation between a man and a woman; indeed they are not about people, but about privation, hope, despair, anger, jealousy, happiness, longing, and a multitude of other moods.[9] "Our fear of misfortune and death is but the word death; our representations of death which have nothing to do with reality."[10]

Grønbech observed ironically that the Hellenist lived in a closed world, that no one could teach him anything, and that he believed himself to be the alpha and omega of history, that the universe was complete for him because he had realized its guiding idea.[11] Grønbech felt that the stoics were making this assumption and therewith showing their overweening egotism.

Moreover, much of what the stoics preached amounted to a plea that a man should be saved from being human. It is, says Grønbech, as if to be a human being were a kind of sickness.[12] And he describes

Seneca's works as a monstrous hospital journal. No wonder then that
man had to be saved. Thus it is that the key word in religion that
arose in Hellenism was "salvation."

III *Paul*

The transition from the study of Hellenism to the book on Paul is
given in the very first paragraph of Grønbech's *Paulus* (1940):
"Around the beginning of the Christian era the world was one empire, not only politically, but also spiritually. The same administration stretched from the Atlantic to the Euphrates; the same thoughts
concerned minds in Rome and Alexandria and all the lesser cities
which rotated about these two metropolises. Nations had disappeared—except for one, Israel—and had been replaced by humanity."[13] In the midst of this world one man attracts attention by virtue
of what Grønbech calls his "passionate personality." This man was
Paul, who belonged to "that class of geniuses who look upon the
universe with themselves as a central point."[14] This characterization
is sufficient to show Grønbech's bias regarding Paul and his unwillingness on the whole to accept Paul as the champion of the ideas
that had been articulated by Jesus.

If one comes to Grønbech's *Paulus* from his *Jesus* with the assumption that *Paulus* is simply the second volume of a trilogy on
early Christianity, one is surprised to discover, first, that the two
books themselves are very different, and, second, that there is an
abyss between Grønbech's Paul and Grønbech's Jesus. On reflection, however, one finds a forthright explanation: Paul was different
from Jesus; but the discrepancy becomes the greater if one accepts,
even only as a working hypothesis, Grønbech's contention that Paul
misunderstood Jesus and was no model Christian. In point of fact,
Grønbech must be called one of Paul's severest critics. He stresses
that Paul did not know Jesus personally and implies that a comparison of the words of Jesus as contained in the first three Gospels with
the writings of Paul is sufficient to demonstrate that Paul was not
reproducing the words of Jesus but instead giving his own interpretation of them. Grønbech identifies Paul's attitudes as naïve. He felt
that Paul resembles the traditional Israelite and that his attitude
reflects more clearly the ethic of the Old Testament than the New.
Paul is both a Jew and a Hellenist. Although he is a synthesis of the
two, in the synthesis the Jew predominates; Grønbech entitles one
of the chapters in his book "The True Israelite." He feels that Paul

shared the weaknesses of Hellenistic culture: "He lacked an harmonious unity; he harbored a fear of life."[15] Grønbech saw in Paul an emotional ascetic and a Hellenistic egoist who was more a champion of the rabbinical tradition than an interpreter of a new pact.

For Grønbech Paul was a representative of Hellenistic culture who set Christianity off on a tangent. Paul's relation to Jesus was, after all, secondhand. He was not one of the twelve apostles, and Grønbech was convinced that had Paul heard Jesus preach, he would have condemned Him as immoral. While Paul believed himself to be the champion of the new faith, his Christianity was an extension of a legalistic Judaism and cannot be deduced from the ideas of Jesus in the New Testament.

Since on the one hand Grønbech is so skeptical of the nature of Paul's contribution to embryonic Christianity and, on the other, the Christian church has to such a large extent developed along the lines indicated by Paul, a reader draws the conclusion that Grønbech is also skeptical of Pauline doctrines, which for him were not to be equated with any metaphysical entity that might be constructed from the words of Jesus in the New Testament. Grønbech in no way attempts to make Paul's historical position or influence seem less important than they have been—for there is no denying Paul's impact on the development of Christianity and the acceptance of his ideas among Christian believers. Nevertheless, Grønbech stresses the contrast between Paul's interpretation of Jesus and Jesus' own teachings. For Grønbech it is as if Paul were utilizing Jesus for his own purposes.

Much of Grønbech's inspired exposition results in his argumentative paraphrasing of the epistles of Paul. While he gives almost no direct references to sources in his text, Grønbech is intimately familiar with all that Paul wrote, and despite his aversion to Paul's misunderstanding of Jesus and despite Paul's egotism, Grønbech is able to speak for Paul just as he was able to identify himself in other works with the figures about whom he wrote. There is no doubt that much of Grønbech's presentation is speculative. His interpretation of the text is necessarily subjective since there is little other evidence besides the texts of the New Testament itself to work with, but Grønbech has got to know Paul so well that he even feels able to sense the tone of Paul's voice. In any case, Grønbech is at all times proffering a fresh interpretation of Paul without resorting to a critical analysis of the vast secondary literature about the figure who

next to Jesus himself is the most important individual in the New
Testament.

Grønbech points out, on the one hand, that Paul is not a mystic
and that in fact mysticism is for him a closed world and, on the
other, that he has a hazy, almost mystical concept of *christos*. For
Paul Jesus is more than the Messiah—but he is not God. *Christos* is
the new law, albeit in the spirit of the law of Israel. Jesus is not
identical to *christos*, for christos is an abstraction; the believer can
accept *christos* and live in *christos*. *Christos* is the death and the
resurrection, and *christos* is also the congregation of the believers.
"In the same breath he can speak about *christos* as a condition and
christos as a person . . . to live is for me *christos* says Paulus, and to
die is an achievement because it means that I am together with
christos."[16]

For Grønbech Paul is the moralist and the theologian of early
Christianity. But Paul's *christos* damns the flesh and hates life. In
Grønbech's opinion, Paul therefore remains rooted in the restrictive
Judaism from which Jesus had extricated himself. Nevertheless
Grønbech unhesitatingly identifies Paul as a genius, since to Paul
the activist, the organizer, the critic, the agitator, more than to any
other person, the organized Christian church owes its genesis and
the direction that its theological speculation took at a very early
date. Grønbech pays particular attention to the struggle that took
place between Paul and the synagogue in Jerusalem. This section of
Paulus is a harbinger of the third volume of the series *Kristus*.
Through his analysis of the Acts of the Apostles and the letters of
Paul, Grønbech is able convincingly to argue that grave tensions
existed between Jerusalem—in which the current within Judaism
that was to become Christianity was wholly dominated by the family
of Jesus—on the one hand, and the strong-minded, legalistic,
epistle-writing traveling apostle on the other.

In contradistinction to the aggressive Paul, whose letters Grønbech views as no less than propagandistic, is set Peter, whom Grønbech looks upon as Paul's antithesis, who lacked Paul's incisive
mind, aggressiveness, and conviction.

Paul's great importance, according to Grønbech, lay in the fact
that he "evoked the religious forces in Hellenism and much against
his will inspired the heathen followers of Christ to independence."[17]

As the Danish clergyman Marius Hansen reminded readers in an
early criticism of the book, Grønbech's *Paulus* is written by a histo-

rian of religion and not by a theologian.[18] The comment was intended pejoratively. Danish men of the cloth were of two minds about Grønbech's *Paulus*, as they were about some other works by Grønbech. There is, however, no doubt that Grønbech was a source of inspiration to many contemporary Danish clergymen. An answer to the negative criticism by Marius Hansen is the review by Knud Hansen, also a clergyman, which begins by stating that although *Paulus* is not written first and foremost for theologians it is "*also* for theologians. Also those theologians who otherwise do not read. . . ." Knud Hansen recognized the radical quality of Grønbech's *Paulus* but took an appreciative and tolerant attitude when he said: "it is more fruitful to read such a book than to read one which only expresses the same opinion that you already possess or says what you could have said yourself." Knud Hansen also makes the brilliant observation in his review[19] (in the journal of the Danish folk-high-school movement) that the Gospels had hitherto regularly been read and understood from Paul's standpoint instead of understanding Paul from the standpoint of the Gospels and letting his place in theology be determined by that understanding.

Grønbech's most outspoken critic was the theologian N. H. Søe. In an article on *Paulus* published in the journal of the society of Danish clergymen Søe wrote: "[I]t is not a sympathetic picture which Grønbech draws of Paul. A torn, fanatically passionate soul plagued by guilt complexes whose life is a constant struggle and who carries on polemics."[20] While this was meant as negative criticism of Grønbech, it is a fairly accurate, although by no means exhaustive, description of Grønbech's image of Paul.

The very restricted appeal of Grønbech's book on Paul (it has not been reprinted) can in part be explained through the fact that Grønbech's mode of writing was different in *Paulus* than in *Jesus*. *Paulus* is difficult in particular because of Grønbech's tendency toward peroration. An early reviewer of the book called it baroque because of Grønbech's tendency to produce endless variations on a principle or observation rather than to carry on a straightforward, logically constructed argumentation. It is not merely a careless criticism to state that the book is sometimes prolix. The effect on the reader may be ascribed in part, however, to the fluidity and melody of Grønbech's language in *Paulus*, the subtlety of his variations on a theme, the insistence of his repetitions, and the diffuseness of his metaphors. One is carried along by the strong rhetorical current of Grønbech's words, in itself a corollary to his conviction that his interpretations are valid.

IV *Messianism*

Whereas *Paulus* is more difficult reading than *Jesus*, the third volume in the trilogy on early Christianity is again more readily comprehensible and seemingly written for a larger audience: *Kristus* is not simply a single argument or a depiction of early Christianity, but a series of individual studies on the rise of Christianity as an organized religion. On the basis of the Gospel according to Luke and the Acts of the Apostles—two books which Grønbech agrees must be considered to complement one another—Grønbech attempts to deduce the history of the first congregations of the followers of Jesus. He makes the point that the earliest congregations were made up of Jews who accepted the tenet that Jesus was indeed the Messiah. Grønbech calls his book *Kristus* because it concerns the messianic belief. *Christos* is the Greek word for Messiah. Proof that Jesus was the Messiah was to be found quite simply in the resurrection; this was the single important element of faith that distinguished the earliest followers of Jesus from other Jews. While Grønbech's interpretation is intuitive, it is based upon a thorough knowledge of the culture of Hellenism, including contemporary Judaism, and with the texts that make up the New Testament.

The first step in depicting the origins of Christianity is to deduce the history of the congregation in Jerusalem. The second is to pay attention to the spread of the messianic belief to congregations elsewhere—from Antioch to Rome—while the pragmatic and complex reasons for the spread of the Christian belief and its acceptance in so many places remain largely a matter of conjecture. The Pauline epistles reflect an effort to guide and contain the development of the new faith which now begins to proselytize and bring satisfaction to many searching souls in the Hellenistic world.

The third step in relating the story of the development of a Christian religion is to look beyond Luke to John, who introduces into the new faith a mystical element that hitherto had been lacking and that could lend it some of the appeal of the various mystery religions of Hellenism and disseminate the idea of the church as the mystical body of Christ: *Christos.*

A fourth and final step is to recognize the rise of legends that embroidered upon and filled out the relatively simple message of

Jesus as contained in the gospels of Matthew, Mark, and Luke. Grønbech lets us understand that the original tradition was considerably extended; and there was a new emphasis upon miracles. The Christian religion of variegated appeal that became a synthesis of many elements both Judaic and non-Judaic assumed roughly the features with which we are familiar today.

In many ways Grønbech is attempting to depict Christianity from the standpoint—specifically the Jewish standpoint—of the times. Jesus is viewed as the Jewish Messiah rather than the incarnation of God. From what little we know about early Christian congregations and about the members of Jesus' family, Grønbech develops a somewhat tenuous history of the struggles to organize a new church in the first decades following the crucifixion of the Master. Here as elsewhere Grønbech argues on the basis of how it must have been, given the cultural situation of the time and the personalities of the individuals involved. He argues that there was a struggle between the apostles and members of Jesus' family, notably Jesus' brother James. Fascinating is Grønbech's endeavor to recapture historically the congregation in Jerusalem and the unrest from which it suffffered because of internal dissension. Grønbech senses what we would now call a power struggle to shape the fate of the early congregations. He assumes early believers in the divinity of Jesus to have been ordinary human beings with ordinary human feelings and ambitions. While some, and perhaps much of his presentation must be considered hypothetical, Grønbech's hypotheses seem reasonably well-founded. The members of the earliest congregations were in conviction and practice Jewish and could not yet be considered Christian in any traditional, modern sense of the term. The formation of groups of believers—early Christians—who were not necessarily Jewish was a secondary development, the history of which can be deduced in part from the Acts of the Apostles and more particularly from the letters of Paul.

Grønbech reminds us that we know nothing about the authors of the Gospels or how they were preserved or rewritten. He remains convinced, however, that the authors of the Gospels felt a charge to preserve sacred tradition and especially to preserve unaltered the words of Jesus. This does not connote, however, that everything in the Gospels is to be interpreted literally. In the Gospel of John, Grønbech feels, we are confronted with an artist or poet who has let his imagination have fairly free rein. John's gospel is, however, important to Grønbech because it provides such a contrast to the ideas of Paul.

Grønbech emphasizes that early Christianity was not yet an independent religion. The Christian religion was in the process of developing and creating a church that gradually became differentiated from organized Judaism. Grønbech does not go into the matter of the acquisition of the many elements that were necessarily fused into Christianity as a system of belief and as an organized church that was in a position first to compete with and then to supplant other religions within the Roman Empire of the first century.

Grønbech's interpretation of Christianity as evinced in *Jesus, Paulus*, and *Kristus* is brilliant and in many ways persuasive but it is also personal and eccentric. There is a visible disregard of much biblical scholarship in the effort to produce a new interpretation of texual material and to dissolve the patina of Holy Writ. As in both *The Culture of the Teutons* and *Hellenism*, Grønbech creates a metaphysical construct that is remarkable for its insights and originality, that contains many truths, but that covers such an expanse of material both topically and chronologically, that one may not asssume the picture Grønbech creates to have absolute or constant validity, even though his individual observations and hypotheses might be accurate enough.

All three volumes are in a way evangelical: they are based upon the testimony of the New Testament, with particular reference to the words of Jesus, and they serve to interpret the New Testament in modern terminology. Each of the three books retells Biblical events. In speaking of these books one runs the risk of attempting a paraphrase of Grønbech, who himself is paraphrasing parts of the New Testament. Because of the stimulating and critical interpretations of Biblical texts that he provides, Grønbech is worth reading, but there is little point in trying to reformulate Grønbech's paraphrases.

Whereas the volume on Hellenism, like the later study of Hellas, may be said basically to use the same method as was employed in *The Culture of the Teutons*, the trilogy on early Christianity does not. To be sure, Grønbech is searching for the basic concepts that inform the words of Jesus and the epistles of Paul, and that were accepted by the early believers, but his approach is here neither as philological nor as detached as in his other works, which deal with cultures from a more objective historical point of view. It is understandably more difficult to be detached about Christianity when one writes in the Christian era and from a Christian standpoint. Rather than dissection and explanation, Grønbech is here given to interpretation and argumentation. He is not disseminating rudimentary information to those who would learn about a distant phenomenon, but is attempting to convince contemporaries who already possess some familiarity with the source material with which he works.

CHAPTER 7

Describing Hellas

I Basic Metaphysical Concepts

THE four-volume study of the culture of Greece entitled *Hellas*, which was published between 1942 and 1945 and was supplemented by an additional volume five years after Grønbech's death, is in concept and execution parallel to *The Culture of the Teutons*. The first volume begins by casting doubt upon archeology as the source of convincing proof of what has happened in the past. Archeological finds Grønbech looked upon only as being a means to enlighten us about extant texts. For him, the word as it has been preserved in writing should be considered the primary and major source of our information about the past. As in *The Culture of the Teutons*, Grønbech searches the vocabulary of an earlier time for those words that are particularly important and that are keys to the basic concepts that informed an older culture. Grønbech was himself aware of the parallelism between his two works and referred frequently to the older study in his interpretation of Greek culture. Some of the chapters have almost identical headings in the monographs. Thus, in the first volume of *Hellas*, which deals with the era of the nobles, there are chapters on "honor and luck" and "life and death"; the titles might have been taken out of *The Culture of the Teutons*. In both studies Grønbech inclines to view a rather long period of time as culturally unified. He does not enter into a discussion of semantic change or differences among the Greek dialects any more than he considered semantic problems in *The Culture of the Teutons*, although he does suggest a transition in religious thought from an older, complex, and naive belief in the many Greek gods toward a less complex, more sophisticated, and ethically modified attitude.

As in his examination of Germanic antiquity, Grønbech stressed certain concepts that he felt lay at the basis of the culture he was dissecting. These concepts cannot be simply translated because of their complex connotations and because they are symbolic of attitudes and convictions that cannot be compressed into a single word. *Kydos*, for example, has no simple equivalent today because the modern languages are, in Grønbech's words, "unable to reproduce an experience which we do not know and cannot sense."[1] In addition to *kydos*, Grønbech discusses a number of other Greek concepts: *kleos*, *timē*, *olbos*, *thymos*, *aidos*, and *dikē*, to mention the most important. Only a few of these concepts, and notably *thymos*, is he able to translate to his own satisfaction. He feels that the terms cannot be understood until one has grasped what they meant in the life of an ancient Greek—or at least an Athenian.

The discussion of individual words is less accessible to the general reader than it was in the earlier work, however, simply because Grønbech is now given to quoting more Greek than he did Old Icelandic. Many of the words with which he deals are known to the educated reader in Western culture, however, because these words have been accepted into the Western languages—as, for example, nemesis, psyche, and hybris; but there are many other words that are not commonly used in English or German or French and that require some knowledge of Greek in order to define and grasp. Understandably, Grønbech avoids attempting to give simple equations in Danish for individual Greek concepts, because many words have such ramifications in their connotations that they are difficult to circumscribe. Not infrequently he evades the issue of translation by using the Greek word or words in a sentence—a method unsatisfactory to the reader who knows little or no Greek. It does not help today's reader to be told that certain words mean more than we now can grasp. This position is philosophically untenable in any case, for words and concepts do not exist outside the human mind, and one may therefore conclude that all words and all concepts are explicable even though the explanations must be detailed and lengthy.

Volume I of *Hellas* is devoted to an examination of the basic concepts of existence in classical Greece, but—again as in *The Culture of the Teutons*—the importance of the family and of familial relationships is stressed. Grønbech's principal sources for his description of the greater family or clan are Homer and Pindar. Despite the parallels that otherwise obtain between *Hellas* and *The Culture of the Teutons* and the fact that the most important concepts with which Grønbech deals are identical in both studies, Grønbech insists that the kinds of reality possessed by the two cultures were different.

Not only are the words that Grønbech elects to define and make representative of ancient Greek culture individual concepts, they are depicted as metaphysical forces possessed of a definable perimeter. That is, they are not merely psychologically colored attitudes; they possess independent, if metaphysical, existence. This is not surprising, however, for the historian of religion works with abstractions—whether they be supernatural powers or metaphysical forces. What a community of human beings has created both individually and separately by observation, discussion, and hypothesis becomes a valid unit and remains such as long as there are believers.

All Grønbech's observations and conclusions are the result of deduction. He has closely examined the monuments of Greek antiquity—both major and minor—and sought to recognize objectively which were the most important ideas of classical society based on its vocabulary. Grønbech tends sometimes to hyperbole, in an effort to emphasize the differences between classical antiquity and today. Thus he writes in discussing *thymos*, for example: "life for us is colourless impersonal energy, which in a mysterious way assumes form or can educe form, wholly personal."[2] Similar sweeping and rather vague statements do not give today's readers a tangible definition.

Homer is for Grønbech the primary source of information and the major point of reference. Five other major writers overshadow all other, but not necessarily lesser, writers (e. g., Aristotle): Aeschylus, Aristophanes, Euripides, Herodotus, and Pindar. Next to Homer, Pindar is Grønbech's most important source in identifying the allusions to ordinary virtues of daily life. Pindar writes occasional poetry, in contrast to the heroic Homerian epic. Grønbech discusses Pindar's poetry at length and in detail, but he never gives the interpretation of an entire poem so that his reader might be able to see the several difficult and nominally characteristic terms that Pindar uses in context.

In the same spirit as in his other earlier works, Grønbech is impressed by the unity of Greek life and by the fact that the early Greek felt himself to be a member of a society. Many of the differences that Grønbech perceives to be made by the modern European were not made by the Greek. Thus, says Grønbech, the difference we feel between soul and body simply did not exist in Greek antiquity and even the concepts of life and death differ. Grønbech observes that the ancient Greek, unlike the modern European, did not live his life in compartments and that the Greek understood his own limitations: "The Greek wanted to do what he was able to do and not what he was unable to do."[3] Grønbech also points out that Greek literature was neither melodramatic nor aesthetically determined. Beauty for the Greek, says Grønbech, was something internal, a part of the whole, and nothing superficial as he felt to be the case in modern art and literature. Incidentally, volume I of *Hellas* is more difficult to read than the following volumes because there are no explanatory chapter headings in the text. There is, however, a table of contents at the back of the book that provides a simple key to the subjects being discussed and thus permits a more rapid perusal of the text than when one is confronted solely by a lengthy argument broken only here and there by Roman numerals.

II The Revolution

There is no effort at a concluding synthesis at the end of volume I. Grønbech has been discussing the role of the family and the clan in Greek life, with Pindar as his witness, and after having attempted to bound the concept *arkhé,* he ceases writing, but at a juncture that leads into the more general social and political discussion of volume II, *The Revolution.*

The "revolution" of Grønbech's second volume on the culture of Hellas is that wrought by the dominance of commerce—a commerce based on the intrinsic value of money. This change from a simple to a more complex, from an agricultural, self-sufficient to a highly organized, commercial society based on an easy means of exchange, seems normal to the modern reader—but it is this very impression that is central to Grønbech's argument: that the Greek fifth century B.C. possessed many parallels to life as we know it today. Grønbech tries to make the events of Greek history both comprehensible and commonplace. This is the one principle that informs *Hellas* II; the other is a principle that one meets time and again in Grønbech— that reality is not stable: reality changes, just as everything else in the world changes with the passage of time. A change of reality can also be revolutionary.

Grønbech's principal witnesses are Herodotus and Plato, and again Pindar and Homer—above all Homer. Grønbech approaches

classical Greek literature not as if it were mere historical ornament
but as living literature. For him Herodotus is "the world's most
fascinating narrator." It requires a penetrating familiarity with the
historical subject and an easy command of the Greek language to
make such a statement. For Grønbech Plato is not only a master of
philosophic, Socratic dialogue, but also a reformer—and Pericles is
seen as a champion of political isolation, whereas Pindar represents
an opposite point of view. The contrasts and tensions of the fifth
century B.C. are those which turn an aristocratic into a democratic
society—that is, which effect a social revolution.

The lengthy discussion of Homer does not mesh well with the
threads that make up the argument in the rest of volume II of
Hellas, for Grønbech engages in a personal interpretation of
Homeric poetry and stresses Homeric imagery and metaphor while
providing many examples cited in translation. Grønbech would refute the hypothesis that Homer is folk poetry or the fusion of several
older and lesser epics. In his opinion Homer or the poets identified
by the term Homer are renewers of poetry who, to be sure, are
working with literary tradition and are not wholly original but who
are not mere instruments of transmission nor voices of the people.
The Homeric poets are rather great artists who can give lasting and
impressive form to known material. The Homeric tales are engendered by poets' fantasy without, however, being fantastic. They are
tall tales, perhaps, but not incredible. Homer—like Pindar or
Theogenes—is necessarily retrospective: "They reveal the depths of
the old aristocratic soul, but at the same time they reveal the emo-
tions which are vented about them and which also are vented within
their own souls."[4] Only at such a time, when the old order changes,
is it possible to acquire the retrospective insight essential to the
creation of such a monument as the Homeric epics. They are themselves not revolutionary, but the revolution is in Grønbech's view a
requisite for their genesis. Thus it is that Grønbech includes his
discourse about Homer in a volume with the subtitle *The Revolution*. The old order acquires dignity and historical patina while the
new burgher must confront ethical problems made acute by the
revolution and, Grønbech lets us understand, no problem is more
demanding than that of the question of what is good and what is bad.
This matter became one of religious speculation—which is the point
of departure for *Hellas* III (1945), *Gods and Men*.

Grønbech would contradict the common assumption that the Hellene of the fifth century B.C. was a human ideal or, as he puts it, "the original human phenomenon." The adulation of the fifth century Greece Grønbech dismisses as a "romantic dogma," for Hellas in the fifth century was in part magnificent—but in part also paltry and wretched. Grønbech felt that one force was now all powerful in society: money. Objects acquired intrinsic value and the strong bonds that had held Greek society together gave way. As Grønbech would have it, with his tendency to employ Greek terms for the concepts he would express, *aidos* slipped out of the world and there was no more *moira*. Grønbech's principal source for this pessimistic canvas of fifth century Greece was Theognis, but the vulgarization of older Greek culture through the rise of commerce and the dominance of money Grønbech suggested by using numerous vulgarisms in discussing the political situation of that time when the Greek state had become bourgeois.

While Grønbech admires Homer, he does not look upon him as a poet of the people but rather as a minstrel who entertained men in power by tales of the distant past. Grønbech is sufficiently taken by Homer's metaphors and similes to devote a number of pages to his own direct translations of picturesque passages in Homer. These he calls a "picture book from Hellas," the Hellas through which Homer walked using his five senses.[5]

It is apparent that Grønbech sees similarities between Europe in the twentieth century and Greece of the fifth century B.C. He is nevertheless cautious about drawing instructive parallels between ancient time and today and warns against them as a misdirection of history. There is nevertheless no denying that he is particularly sensitive to those aspects of existence in ancient Greece that bear comparison with aspects of life today.

III *Gods and Men*

The third volume of *Hellas* reverts to the method of volume I by attempting definitions and explanations of various important words with religious significance, particularly the terms *aidos* and *sebas*. Grønbech has carefully researched many Greek sources in order to find evidence of the practice of religion in Greek antiquity. He does not believe that any common religion can be seen to have existed in all Greek states but he is able to perceive and define a Hellenic religion in Athens. Curiously enough, his most important source turns out to be Aristophanes because of the many casual references to religious usage found in Aristophanes' plays.

This volume on "gods and men" is almost eclectically anecdotal; the reader is confronted with much factual information and much critical interpretation. While briefer, individual sections of the volume are easily comprehensible, the sum total of material and interpretation makes demanding reading. The use of Greek terms in his text makes the transmission of Grønbech's own ideas to the reader rather difficult. The overall presentation is made less lucid by the lack of a table of contents—doubtless merely an oversight—not to mention the lack of an index. The reader must laboriously establish an outline of the volume as he works his way through the text.

Grønbech lays particular stress on the festival and on what he identifies as ritual drama. Rather unexpectedly, he now draws upon archeology for evidence to support his views to the extent of reproducing three sections of frieze by line drawings in the text, although he reassures his readers that, as welcome as artifacts and documents are, they provide pragmatic information and they do not suffice to write the history of religion, or indeed of life as it was lived in the past. "We first get to know life by listening to the testimony of living men about what they experienced," he writes.[6] Grønbech sees the most dependable evidence in prose and verse, even when preserved only fragmentarily, although admittedly the proper interpretation of such poetic evidence is demanding.

The argument for the existence and importance of ritual drama is constructed from bits and pieces of evidence. Similarly, Grønbech establishes hypotheses about certain other rituals of a religious nature in Athenian society, notably the ritual pertaining to eating and drinking as suggested by casual evidence scattered throughout classical Greek literature.

Here as elsewhere in his works, Grønbech is interpreting ritual drama of which he now gives a poignant and striking description: its fundamental substance is the overcoming of the power of evil by the—combined—efforts of gods and men, although the religious standpoints of the human participants may be different, so different indeed that Grønbech would speak of at least two religions in Hellas: on the one hand the religion of the aristocrat, and on the other, of the peasant.[7] In a supplement to volume III of *Hellas*, which was published in volume V in 1953, Grønbech endeavors to describe the peasant culture and its religion which, he suggests, is a reflection of the rhythm of life. That is to say, Grønbech seems here to be approaching the older concept of fertility rites as the origin of organized religion. This tendency is reinforced in the second supplement, entitled "The Gods" (also published in volume V), in which ritual and other religious acts are interpreted symbolically. One should bear in mind that the final, English, and thus the canonical version of *The Culture of the Teutons* was augmented by a chapter on the ritual drama.

If there is one leitmotif in volume III of *Hellas* it is that in classical Greece there was no discrepancy between religion and life, between the religious and the worldly. Religion was simply identical with culture—a state of affairs that seems to be in striking contrast to the twentieth century in the West. This matter of the interrelationship of religion and daily life is, of course, of lasting and central importance to Grønbech and is the subject of his perorations time and again. He was repeatedly attracted to cultures where he sensed a unity of religion and practical life and where the individual partook of the religious community. Indeed, as we have observed before, he saw in such relationships a desirable and an achievable ideal.

At the beginning of the third volume Grønbech makes a more incisive comment directed at our own times when he speaks in the same fashion as he did at the beginning of *Religious Currents* in 1922. Religion, he says, "has long since lost its significance—that is, all practical reality—so it would occur to no one that the divine might intervene actively in our daily dispositions; no one would seriously believe that a religious argument could be employed parallel with practical reasons in order to determine legislation or social arrangements."[8]

Since volume III of *Hellas* concerns itself primarily with the practice of religion in daily life and the implications of religion for daily life, it is not surprising that Grønbech makes a number of generalities regarding religion throughout the volume. Time and again he suggests the interdependence of religion and daily life in a culture where there is an effective religion and consequently a high, unified culture. Such statements as "religion is to live life completely, life in all its fullness and force" or "the religion of antiquity concerns man from first to last and not only his soul"[9] or "religion consists in life being directed to its highest possibilities"[10] must be considered oblique commentary on the role of religion in modern

European society where the very unity that Grønbech sees in
Athens and the fullness of life that is permeated by religious conviction, ritualism, and symbolism is lacking. Grønbech projects no
dream of a golden age, for the society that he describes in Athens is
not an ideal one and is by no means without the ordinary human
failings that guarantee flaws in any society. Nevertheless, he is
suggesting that the philosophical and ethical—or, if one will,
religious—quality of life in classical Athens deserves admiration if
not emulation. "Religion is life at its highest point"[11] he opines, and
without a religion comparable to that of classical Athens man does
not achieve that pinnacle that otherwise might be his.

Perhaps somewhat unexpectedly, Aristophanes becomes Grønbech's crown witness, since he finds that he provides the best mirror
of Athenian daily life. Grønbech even employs Aristophanes as a
major witness about the religious festivals of Athens and, by means
of many quotations, albeit in translation, Grønbech tries to give the
reader insight into various aspects of the—religious—festival, the
festival which, he explains, was "the highest realism"[12] and was
prophetic. Grønbech describes the important elements of the festival as best he can, with his usual effort to designate and define
certain glosses as fundamental to the Greek concept of the interpretation of reality. The abundance of Greek expressions, although
Grønbech undertakes to explain them as they occur, are difficult for
a reader to absorb and retain unless he is at home in Attic Greek.

IV   Thinkers and Playwrights

The fourth volume of *Hellas* is different not only from the other
three volumes of the series but also from Grønbech's other works. It
falls into three parts: The first section is devoted to an interpretive
and paraphrastic discussion of the extant fragments of the writings of
ancient Greek thinkers. The second part, dealing with the bourgeois
culture of Athens and the plays of Aeschylus and Sophocles, is much
nearer to conventional literary history than Grønbech was wont to
write. The third part is a study of Euripides, but consists to a considerable extent of selections from Euripides translated into Danish.

The volume begins with a discussion of Heraclitus—essentially a
repetition of Grønbech's presentation contained in the second volume of Mystics. This is the third time that he wrote about Heraclitus. A discussion follows of Xenophanes and Pythagoras who, like
Heraclitus, is considered by Grønbech to have been a mystic. Em-

pedocles, however, Grønbech identifies as a prophet. Heraclitus, Xenophanes, and Pythagoras interest Grønbech because they are representatives of a great and fruitful period of conflict and contradiction in the fifth century B.C.; they exude a spirit of revolution, for they were trying to reconstruct the world—albeit from the standpoint of the individual rather than of society. Unlike them, Empedocles gives evidence of having conceived an internal harmony. Grønbech does not envisage Empedocles as possessing an optimistic attitude toward life; on the contrary, he feels that Empedocles identifies the greatest forces in the world as love and hatred, those forces on which all creatures draw in order to live. Nevertheless, Empedocles senses a balance and pattern in existence that suggest the prerequisites of harmony.

The fragments that have been preserved of the work of Pythagoras and Empedocles fired Grønbech's imagination and caused him to write in an elevated and introspective style—a striking contrast to the down to earth historical dialogue he employs in drawing on Plato while discussing the situation of the Athenian citizen. In the latter case there is a clear overtone of Copenhagen commonplace, the slightly vulgar colloquial speech one might have heard on the streets of the Danish capital about the time Grønbech was writing. This sudden descent from the rhetorical to the everyday jolts the reader into a realization that the "problems of life" that are being discussed are not far removed from us: they resemble such problems as confront every man—but the social and more especially the religious context is different. Aeschylus is looked upon as a wholly realistic writer who accepted the existence of the Greek pantheon of gods unquestioningly. The religious and ethical questions reflected and depicted in the plays are the great problems of life, if the basic assumptions of Greek religion are made. There is a gradual social change:—the shift of power from the family—or the clan—to the state; but ultimately—the matter is one of fundamental assumptions and convictions—that is, of religion.

Grønbech seems to be titillated by the problem of divining a system of thought implied by philosophical fragments from the past that are in themselves stimulating. He is convinced that Heraclitus and Empedocles, different as the two were, each partook of another reality that was unlike our own. Indeed, this seems to be a driving force in all of Grønbech's investigations. Whether he is dealing with a culture of the past or the ineffable world of the mystic, he is

captivated by the idea that a dynamic metaphysical reality different
from the reality in which Western man functions can exist. He finds
it the foremost task of a historian of religion to be able to perceive
and to penetrate another reality and to accept its existence upon the
same plane with the reality that he knows from everyday existence.
It is quite possible that the existence of various bits and fragments
that give evidence of a different *Weltanschauung* makes Grønbech
ply his imagination more vigorously than were an entire systematic
Weltanschauung preserved and visible. At the same time Grønbech
warns of the temptation to create an entire system on the basis of
mere fragments. His efforts are both stimulating and tenuous.

As in so many of his other works, Grønbech tends to identify
himself with the subject, so that in the case of Empedocles it is only
partially possible to extricate one writer from the other. The comments occasionally and inevitably tend toward criticism of the present, and one is uncertain whether Grønbech himself is speaking or
letting Empedocles speak for him. For example, he writes: "[M]ost
people are so befuddled by their own senses that they reflect only
dully. They are walled within their own little world so that they
believe the limited accidental experiences they have had endow
them with worldly wisdom. During their brief span of years they are
able to observe only a small part of life; then they are gone like the
fog. Everything they sense is accidental and piecemeal but in their
blindness they assume these scraps to be a whole."[13] While Empedocles may have conceived the thought, this formulation is Grønbech's.

The heart of volume IV is the chapter entitled "The Bourgeois"—
it might be more accurate to say "the citizens"—which involves a
critical discussion of the tragedies of Aeschylus. Grønbech acknowledges that the reforms in Athens that could create a bourgeois state
were the work of aristocrats—but the future that they brought about
belonged to the plebians. "It was these new people, the citizens,
who established a new structure of society religiously and ethically
as well as politically," Grønbech states at the beginning of his discussion.[14] He elects to use Plato's dialogue "Euthyphron" as a
means of introducing the reader to the new bourgeois society. He
does not simply give a translation or a summary of the dialogue,
however, but according to his own admission rewrites—the Danish
word is *gendigte*—the dialogue. In so doing, he makes Plato seem
wittier and more ironic than in the original. Moreover, the dialogue

is recreated in a modern idiom so that the reader can feel the effect of the dialogue as it perhaps was received when originally written. There is no separate interpretation of the text; the interpretation lies in Grønbech's own reworking of the original.

In his treatment of Aeschylus, whom he depicts critically, but from the standpoint of the historian of religion, Grønbech is for once not paraphrastic. Grønbech stands in awe of Aeschylus because in the Greek dramatist the tragedy already has perfected form. The theater is important because it is of religious origin and the great dramas of Greek antiquity were, in Grønbech's opinion, still rooted in religion. Although the myths themselves had lost their force, intrinsically they were important raw material for the dramatist and they permitted him to communicate with theatergoers and to deal with those terms of religious significance that were basic to Athenian culture. Despite the usefulness of the gods and of traditional religious concepts to the writer of tragedy, misfortune in Aeschylus really comes from within. This fact makes Aeschylus a modern dramatist. Grønbech suggests that Aeschylus grasped the eternal laws of human existence, which transcend religious and social systems that have superseded one another in the course of time. Despite the postulated existence of gods from whom emanate evil and good forces, the individual in Aeschylus bears the responsibility for his own deeds.

Here as elsewhere, Grønbech feels that he sees what others have not seen in the past. Consequently, he believes his interpretations to supersede those of earlier critics and scholars. Actually this position is inevitable to every new generation that would undertake a partial revision of viewpoint and interpretation of the past or some element of the past. Grønbech is ironically skeptical of both imaginative writers and critics whose ideas about Greek antiquity and specifically Athens were accepted in the nineteenth century. He feels, for example, that Goethe and Shelley both misunderstood Aeschylus' *Prometheus*. He questions the validity of the school of Max Müller and all those classical philologists whose pedantic exactitude kept them from perceiving the most profoundly motivating ideas in Athenian society at the time of Aeschylus. Thus Grønbech thinks that in *The Seven against Thebes* Aeschylus was articulating a contemporary problem: the collision between the feeling for the clan and the demands of the state. He explains that Aeschylus is suggesting the arbitrary quality of law when society's law emasculates the clan's law. There is a case of right pitched against honor, as is portrayed in Aeschylus' trilogy, the *Oresteia*. The breaking of a law becomes more important than unfaithfulness toward the honor—the *moira*—of the clan. In his recurrent and insistent demand for harmony, Grønbech suggests that Aeschylus points to a lost harmony in which the gods demanded whole-hearted submission from the human being. In Aeschylus' time, we can conclude, there must have been a new god-concept, if only because Aeschylus believed in a just Zeus. This was a different reality from the ancient reality and a religious conviction that to a certain extent presages acceptance of the Judeo-Christian God.

Grønbech's tendency to independent evaluation is marked in his attitude toward Aristotle, of whom he tends to be critical, as is especially noticeable in Grønbech's note dealing with the Pythagoreans.[15] He speaks of Aristotle's "limitations" and dogmatic predilections. Grønbech was of the opinion that Aristotle did not recognize and could not recognize anything but his own system; therefore he had to reject all opinions that could not be classified within his categories. Incidentally, in the criticism contained in the notes to his text, Grønbech evinces familiarity with secondary literature in English and German. For example, he cites John Burnet's *Early Greek Philosophy*, W. K. C. Guthrie's *Orpheus and the Greek Religion*, and works by Jane Ellen Harrison.

Grønbech writes: "In the plays of Aeschylus it is not the struggle of human beings and their reconciliation, their victories and defeats, which are depicted; there is discussed the fate of man; moral problems are debated; solutions are sought to the conflicts of human life; those moods are displayed which are created by fate and world working in unison; the fears and hopes of suffering human beings are clothed in plastic form."[16]

The great appeal that Aeschylus has for Grønbech is suggested by another quotation at the end of his discussion of Aeschylus: "By writing about realities and portraying them to their full extent, Aeschylus leads men to an actuality which exists beneath the realities, to show that the problem does not lie in the order of the universe but in the fact that human beings refuse to see actuality as it is and to live according to it. For this reason his dramas are part of eternal poetry."[17]

This stress of the discrepancy between man's reality at a given time and in a given situation with actuality is a familiar one to

Grønbech's readers by now. Time and again we have observed his acceptance of a multiple reality and his suggestion that several realities can be born by actuality. Here, then, in the classical world, is the same basic matter that has informed Grønbech's examination of man's religion since the first volume of *The Culture of the Teutons* almost four decades previously. One may safely speak of an underlying vein in Grønbech's thought and writings.

Aeschylus is for Grønbech only a historical source of information about religious belief and social structure. There is no concern with Aeschylus the dramatist in any dramaturgical sense. There is no evaluation of drama—its form, devices, or poetic language. That is, any analysis that smacks of aesthetic criticism is absent; there is no effort made to explain the prestige that Aeschylus gained in his own time or the preeminent position he enjoys in the history of drama. For Grønbech, only the ideas that inform Aeschylus are important. Viewing Aeschylus retrospectively, however, in his study of Sophocles, Grønbech does indeed make some comments about Aeschylus' scenic and dramatic realism.

His treatment of Sophocles is unlike that of Aeschylus, for Grønbech sees in them contrasting poets: Sophocles is interested in individuals, while Aeschylus depicts a group or society. Grønbech stresses Sophocles' ability to portray individuals and makes his point by discussing the treatment by those dramatists of the story of Antigone. Grønbech does point out Sophocles' use of scenic devices and melodramatic effects. For Grønbech Sophocles is no mere representative of life and thought—or of unspoken religious assumptions—but rather the skillful dramatic poet who creates characters with easily distinguishable personalities. At one juncture Grønbech reproduces a passage from Sophocles—King Kreon's conversation with a messenger bringing ill tidings—in the commonplace language that he had also used in reproducing a Platonic dialogue. Where he is able to do this with a literary classic, he is himself much taken by the work's lasting validity and convincing reality. Thus he writes, "[I]n Aeschylus we get a picture of human beings struggling for life and grasping for that which is best and truest" while "Sophocles depicts human beings as they are."[18] Grønbech felt that Aeschylus was depicting the classical Athenian Greek, while Sophocles was depicting the modern, urban Athenian.

Grønbech's essay on Euripides is nearly an antithesis to the essay on Aeschylus, for Euripides is the subject of lengthy critical analysis

with special reference to Euripides' depiction of character. Grønbech identifies Euripides as a psychological dramatist in the first
instance and as the author of sensational drama in the second.
Grønbech finds Euripides to be the realist among the three Greek
dramatists he is discussing and claims somewhat unexpectedly that
it would occur to nobody to apply the term "realism" to Aeschylus or
Sophocles—although earlier in volume IV of *Hellas* he seemed to
describe Aeschylus as a realistic writer.

Grønbech opines that the principal difference between Sophocles
and Euripides is that Sophocles was interested in human beings as
human beings, whereas Euripides was interested solely in psychic
phenomena. Such clear-cut categorization may certainly be questioned, as may not a few of Grønbech's other judgments that verge
on the pontifical. The authoritative and often debatable—judgments
are counterbalanced by the mass of detail that Grønbech supplies,
including many passages translated from the Greek that permit the
reader to make many observations for himself and thereby to test
the validity of many of Grønbech's more sweeping statements.

The essay on Euripides more nearly resembles traditional literary
history than much, indeed most, of what Grønbech wrote, for here
one finds the recapitulation and abstraction, consideration, quotation, and the précis of plots. Like most literary history, however,
the Euripides essay is demanding and difficult reading for the
reader who has only a superficial acquaintance with the subject.
One had best read Euripides first before trying to test the texture of
Grønbech's argument; otherwise a wealth of allusions and references is lost, and the essay may seem to be a jumble of too many
facts, hypotheses, and quotations with which Grønbech would recall
to his reader's mind scenes and characters in Euripides.

Incidentally, Grønbech does not withhold his negative criticisms
of Euripides; he finds the Greek given to pathos and melodrama. To
demonstrate his point Grønbech retells many scenes from the
dramas—in particular the drama *Ion,* with the many confrontations
between Kreousa and her long-lost son Ion. But here, too,
Euripides evokes catharsis in his audience. He is, concludes Grønbech, "the pioneer of aesthetic feeling"—but this is a double-edged
remark, coming from Grønbech.

V   The Light from the Acropolis

The reader is perhaps disappointed or perhaps only surprised to
find that the fourth volume of *Hellas* ends without a summary, a

recapitulation, or a conclusion. A volume of notes was to follow (and did in 1953), but the fourth and concluding volume of Grønbech's presentation of ancient Greek culture ends—one could say simply breaks off—with the discussion of Euripides. There are, to be sure, many general observations scattered throughout the four volumes of *Hellas,* generalities that one could assemble in order to review and clarify Grønbech's overall position vis-à-vis the culture of Athens. This is, however, a labor that few readers would take upon themselves. It was therefore fortuitous that circumstance preserved a series of lectures on ancient Greek culture which Grønbech held during the winter of 1943–44 in Copenhagen, for these lectures—*Lyset fra Akropolis (The Light from the Acropolis)*—were not directed to university students but to the broad public that found solace and succor in Grønbech's words during the dark years of the occupation during World War II. Moreover, the style of the lectures brings us close to Grønbech as a speaker, since they were given without reference to a manuscript and were taken down stenographically. Unlike *Hellas,* the lectures comprised a presentation that embraces an introduction and a conclusion as well as a discussion of various important facets of ancient Greek culture. Especially welcome to the reader of *Hellas* are Grønbech's generalizations in the final lecture, for here is the summation that was lacking in the four-volume study, although in a simplified form and in a style different from the more scholarly work. Since Grønbech was speaking to a general audience, where interpretation was difficult and translation were bound to be imprecise, he could not take refuge in a large number of Greek words.

Grønbech's attraction to Greek culture needs no esoteric explanation. He realized, as does every educated person in Western civilization, that our culture is unthinkable without the achievements of Greece in the fifth century B.C. We have but to look about us to observe visible elements of the Greek heritage in buildings and monuments. The European languages are indebted to Greek for innumerable words. Our philosophers take their point of origin in ancient Greek philosophy. Epistomologically we cannot be extricated from ancient Greece. There is, of course, nothing original or unusual about these observations. More important for Grønbech, however, was the fact that the Greeks possessed a myth and that they partook of a common religion that was not a religion of the individual. From Grønbech's earlier works one is aware of the importance to him of a shared faith and of the acceptance of a common myth. He chooses to depict the greatness of Greece in part because Greece did not consist of a society of individualists and was able to carry on religious festivals in which all citizens could gather to celebrate the life and the eternity that their myth granted them. Because Greek existence was permeated by a mutually shared religion, there was in Grønbech's opinion no basic spiritual discrepancy between rich and poor. To him this was an ideal sort of egalitarianism that did not require more practical social and economic equality among individuals. Despite their many internal differences, Greeks shared the common art and the common poetry that gave their society its peculiar strength. In Grønbech's opinion this state of affairs provides a contrast to the current society, which is falling to pieces about us "because every human being is the smith of his own fortune. But by hammering out his own fortune he has smashed society to bits."[19] And modern times no longer understands a myth, says Grønbech, because life for us no longer amounts to visions but merely to precepts. Had it not been for Greek philosophy and religiosity, albeit in the Hellenistic form, the new myth that was Christian theology could not have arisen, Grønbech stressed in the final public lecture. Present-day Christianity was, Grønbech points out, a mixture of Jewish, Hellenistic, and Roman elements, but it grew in the soil of Hellenistic Rome. Some of its elements, notably stoicism, were derived from Hellas. "If I should express with a picture what happened," Grønbech explained, "it would be that a new myth was created."[20]

Grønbech interpreted the demise of Hellas to be the result of the degeneration of Greek religion. He found that the weakness was derived in part from what he called "state egoism": the country consisted of independent city-states, and the citizens of these city-states no longer felt a common bond with the citizens of other city-states; on the contrary, they attempted to exploit each other. This meant, in Grønbech's words, that their god was dead. The phrase is the more striking in Grønbech's final lecture on Greek culture because it reminds us of his criticism of modern times as he had formulated it at the beginning of *Religious Currents in the Nineteenth Century* in 1922—and also because such a precise diagnosis was lacking in the four volumes of *Hellas*. This demise did not mean the destruction of Hellas but rather the introduction of bitterness into Hellenic culture and the creation of a beauty that was tragedy, "for one knew that it led to destruction. One no longer found the eternal in those forms in which one's forefathers had found it; the pleasure of meeting the gods upon the mountain had become almost an empty custom and the Greeks did not succeed in finding God anew in a guise which corresponded to the times."[21]

It has been noted before that Grønbech was a synthesist and that his works tend to be résumés. This observation is strikingly true in the case of *Lyset fra Akropolis*. Grønbech here attempts not only a synthesis and résumé of ancient Greek culture but a synthesis and resumé of his own earlier examination of that culture in *Hellas* I–IV. The lectures are essentially summaries and simplifications of the subjects to which Grønbech addressed himself in *Hellas*. Single lectures are devoted to Aeschylus, Heraclitus, Socrates, Plato, Sophocles, Euripides, and Aristophanes. One notes that Heraclitus is now the only representative of the pre-Socratic philosophers. This fact emphasizes the peculiar position that Heraclitus enjoyed in Grønbech's eyes, although there are few fragments preserved from Heraclitus. That he treats of the other authors mentioned is merely a matter of course. Noteworthy is the fact that Grønbech's final lecture at the University of Copenhagen, given in 1943, also dealt with Hellenic culture, but was more a personal confession, drawing upon his own reminiscences of a visit to Greece, than an attempt at any scholarly analysis. The final lecture ended with a curious turn of phrase that may well have been tempered by the mood of Danish resistance to the wartime occupation. As Grønbech symbolically departs from Acropolis, he feels that he now knows what life has to offer and he is overcome by a giddy feeling of security: "the security that life is so important, so living, that it can afford to be lost."[22] The Acropolis has in the last analysis been for Grønbech the most important sanctuary.

CHAPTER 8

Personal Opinions

I Essays in Relevance

IN most of his works Vilhelm Grønbech employs his peculiar manner of identifying himself with the subject and—apparently—depicting it sympathetically, so that the reader is uncertain of Grønbech's own standpoint and personal evaluation. In more general essays written for a wider audience, however, Grønbech expresses his own opinion directly, without assuming the role of some historical figure. A first collection, which embraces essays from the years 1912–1930, was published in 1930 under the title *Kampen om Mennesket (The Struggle for the Human Being)*. In it Grønbech expresses his own convictions clearly and forcefully; the collection must not be overlooked if one would deduce Grønbech's own attitudes regarding the world around him. He addresses himself to such currently relevant subjects as reading in modern society, the position of scholarship vis-à-vis everyday life, and the significance of the women's movement and the labor movement in the early twentieth century. While the best known of the essays is probably the comparison of the two leading religious figures of nineteenth century Denmark, Søren Kierkegaard and N. F. S. Grundtvig, none is more incisive and at the same time indicative of Grønbech's view of the present state of man than the first essay in the collection, "On Reading," which had originally been published in a Danish periodical *(Gads danske Magasin)* in 1922. Stilistically, "On Reading" reminds one of the beginning of *Religious Currents*, which also appeared in 1922. The concluding sentence of the essay summarizes Grønbech's message: "Reading is in truth a sacred art for man today, for through it we achieve citizenship in the human race and therefore there is a reason in what might otherwise seem to be an odd principle that reading and writing are the beginnings of culture."[1]

118

"The chief function of modern culture," Grønbech avers, "is to encourage the desire to read and give people the means to engender a love of the printed word."[2] Grønbech is convinced that the book has become what he calls the talisman of life. It provides the path the human being must follow to penetrate the surrounding world. It is the means of communication between lonely individuals. In earlier times there was a narrative literature that was the common property of an entire people or a race, and poetry provided the renewal of an experience for the members of a people or a community. Imaginative literature created no suspense for them comparable to that engendered in reading a modern novel; it represented, rather, a fraternal sacrament. Now, however, poetry is no longer a meeting of kin who share common feelings, but "the revelation of unknown events that have taken place in the souls of strangers."[3] Modern society, Grønbech does not tire of saying, consists of a mass of individuals: "We children of modern times have no spiritual life in common. . . . We do not see beyond the individual and for this reason we really have no history."[4] Since the strong feeling of belonging to some community of believers was dissipated in any case by the end of the eighteenth century, the ideal and goal of life since then has been to become a personality. People no longer feel themselves to be involved in any festive act—that is, to be part and parcel of ceremonies—unless it be in the church service, which, Grønbech felt, does preserve a remnant of communality. And in modern times "so natural is this isolation that we hesitate to reveal what transpires within us."[5] We hide it, he points out, behind irony, riducule, and nonchalance. As a consequence, written literature has acquired the function of connecting soul with soul and enabling one individual to experience another. Today one writes what one hesitates to say. Moreover, modern lyric poetry provides in its rhythm and melody means that may be manipulated by the writer so that his communication becomes the more personal. The epic—the major imaginative genre of an earlier society—has all but disappeared and been supplanted by the novel, which is basically a confession and in which an author reveals his own spiritual life. In modern literature the poet can express various facets of his own being by the different characters he elects to put into his work; he can assume roles all the way from Faust to Mephistopheles.

"Books lift modern man out of his lonely imprisonment" in Grønbech's opinion, and in so doing give man access to a society of souls.

In books the reader finds friends who think thoughts he is accustomed to harbor.

The principle that Grønbech expresses in this essay is a radical one—and at loggerheads with Grundtvig's concept of "the spoken word" as the major and ideal avenue of communication among human beings. It is therefore the more curious that Grønbech expresses admiration for Grundtvig, whom in 1930 (in an article on his deceased predecessor Edvard Lehmann) he called the greatest man in the history of Danish intellectual life. Grønbech himself was an effective public speaker who made an indelible impression upon his hearers and could sway them as much as any of his academic contemporaries. Nevertheless, it is difficult to dispute Grønbech's thesis of the importance of the printed word in our time, since any serious discussion of a man's ideas—including Grønbech's—is most often based not upon what he has said but upon what he has written. Even an evaluation of a scholar is difficult—if not impossible—to make on the basis of oral pronouncements, and he tends to be judged by others on the basis of his publications.

On the surface one might not expect Grønbech to be especially sympathetic to the nineteenth century Danish theologian, educator, and agitator N. F. S. Grundtvig, if only because as stylists they are so far removed from one another. Grønbech was, however, able to express considerable admiration for Grundtvig, in particular insofar as he could be looked upon as the antithesis of Søren Kierkegaard. Grønbech was attracted by Grundtvig's insistence on the necessity of a belief shared by a community of believers, a belief that he identified by the same word Grønbech used: myth.

Although Grønbech looked upon Grundtvig as epigonic, he also looked upon him as a prophetic figure who both expressed the needs of the present and suggested some of the developments that were to take place in the twentieth century. Indeed, Grønbech even suggests that a parallel of the unity of belief for which Grundtvig expressed a longing in the early nineteenth century was to be found in the labor movement of the twentieth.

In the essay on Kierkegaard and Grundtvig (which was first published in a Danish newspaper the same year it was reprinted in *Kampen om Mennesket,* 1930), Grønbech writes about the two Danish giants of the nineteenth century: "When one has met them one is overcome by uncertainty. One's attitude toward them is like that of the Greek who has viewed the mysteries: he went away wondering about himself."[6]

Grønbech expressed himself on Kierkegaard a number to times, and, consistently, pejoratively. In the above-mentioned essay, he described Kierkegaard as "the last offshoot of medieval mysticism and its selfish concerns and the scholasticism which was identified with it." For Kierkegaard, said Grønbech, only one thing existed in the whole world, to wit, Kierkegaard's own soul.[7] In that soul everything took place; its feelings and moods and thoughts were life, whereas the surrounding universe acquired reality only in so far as it reflected Kierkegaard's own mind or was drawn into it. For Grønbech, Kierkegaard was too retrospective and was enamored of a culture that was passé—whereas Grundtvig was looking forward to a new realm beyond both Protestantism and Catholicism. Grønbech felt that Kierkegaard's affliction was modern man's affliction, for whom religion had become something quite personal: the individual was concerned only with his own relationship to God or with care for his own soul—as Grønbech put it in an interview with the Copenhagen newspaper *Nationaltidende* on 17 March 1929.

Kierkegaard was felt to represent the kind of mysticism that Grønbech rejects: the self-centered concern associated with Ruysbroek and numerous other medieval figures. Grønbech saw in Kierkegaard the last representative of medieval mysticism for the very reason that Kierkegaard's concern was with himself and with the salvation of his own soul without an understanding for the necessity of a community of believers if human society is to achieve an harmonious state. Grønbech must have read Kierkegaard carefully and doubtless learned much from him, but in the last analysis he rejected Kierkegaard and Kierkegaard's private metaphysical world. It must have been a thorn in the older Grønbech's side to observe the attention Kierkegaard was winning throughout the world in the twentieth century and the role that he played in the developing existential philosophy of the 1940s. Kierkegaard was, of course, not so much a solution for the time as a phenomenon of the time. The intense interest in Kierkegaard and his introspective theology merely emphasized the lack of social harmony that had pervaded Europe in the twentieth century and the forces that drove individuals from one another to think individually rather than to work and act in concert.

It is quite possible that Grønbech's interest in Grundtvig is something of a reaction against Kierkegaard. Since Grundtvig was what
Kierkegaard was not, Grønbech was necessarily more sympathetically inclined toward him. Much in Grundtvig could be forgiven,
because he was ever looking beyond himself and endeavoring to
establish a community of scholars or believers or patriots. Grundtvig
thought in larger entities than did Kierkegaard.

In the essay on Kierkegaard and Grundtvig, Grønbech makes a
remarkable observation: "If one is to speak about Grundtvig's religion, there is no point in starting with what he meant and taught;
one must examine the way he lived and wrote. Nor does it serve a
purpose to describe the elements of his teaching in logical order;
first and foremost, one must sense his poetic work as something
intrinsic, look upon it as a vision, and then undertake to recreate
it."[8] The remark is noteworthy, for Grønbech uses this very method
himself—although never applied to Grundtvig. In fact, he never
wrote anything else about Grundtvig, whom he called a prophet
who belongs to another time—born a thousand years too late.

Grønbech's discussion of the women's movement and the labor
movement in the essay that gave the book its title—"The Struggle
for the Human Being"—dates back to the year 1922 and gives evidence both of clear thinking and an ability to slough off traditional
prejudices. He spoke up for women's rights decades before the
feminist movement of the twentieth century approached a climax,
for he saw in the women's movement, as in the labor movement, a
kind of communality and shared belief for which he was always
pleading. It was not only the injustices involved in the suppression
of women and of the laborer in the late nineteenth and early twentieth centuries that attracted Grønbech's attention, but the ability of
a new grouping of individuals, whether they be women or laborers,
or women and laborers, to organize and be held together by a
common bond of sincere conviction.

Grønbech looked upon the women's movement and the labor
movement as evidence of the purification of society that might improve the future of the Western world. He was, however, no Utopian and did not believe that here or elsewhere perfect harmony
would be achieved for any length of time for, as he said, the actual
achievement of harmony, although a goal for which he always spoke,
would probably be boring and serve to set men off in some new
direction.

II *Essays in Myth*

Kampen for en ny sj'l (The Struggle for a New Soul, 1946*)* both is
and is not another collection of essays by Grønbech. The book had a
curious genesis. A very similar work by Grønbech entitled *Kampen
för en ny själ* appeared in Swedish in 1940. The Swedish version
comprised in part material from Grønbech's volume on the *Religious Currents in the Nineteenth Century* and the first collection of
essays *Kampen om mennesket.* The Swedish book was a translation
from Grønbech's manuscript made by Honorine Hermelin, who was
to become Grønbech's second wife. It was apparently intended as an
introduction to Grønbech's world of thought for a larger Swedish
audience; and it did in any case fulfill this function, for it soon ran
through three printings. The new material contained in the Swedish
volume plus an additional chapter (which had been published in
Sweden in 1942) made up the Danish version issued in 1946. Both
the Swedish and the Danish versions are of particular interest if one
wishes to get closer to Grønbech's own convictions than one ordinarily can when Grønbech writes historically and synthetically—but
only the Danish version is germane to our present discussion, since
the material that was omitted from the Danish version has already
been discussed. The various chapters of *Kampen for en ny sjæl,*
although apparently independently conceived, share a goodly
number of ideas and are welded together by several chapter headings suggestive of Dante's *Commedia.* The ideas that Grønbech
would propagate here are in part similar to those contained in *Religious Currents.* Grønbech's principal argument is that the Renaissance and the Reformation do not constitute a break with the Middle Ages but are a necessary consequence of medieval thought, and
that the great spiritual change in Western civilization came about at
the end of the eighteenth century. He stresses that for the Middle
Ages the dominant myth was that of the pilgrim wending his way
through life toward a better life in the hereafter. As a consequence,
the literature of Europe looked away from everyday life, aspiring
toward the eternal and the infinite. While Grønbech could not subscribe to this myth, he acknowledges the existence of the myth and
its strength and intimates that without some myth life is unsatisfactory. He was later to ask poignantly whether our own century would
discover its own myth—myth that might also be called dogma. The
deplorable aspect of the medieval myth was that its concern ultimately was with the individual and the soul of the individual.

Grønbech felt that Dante, Bunyan, and Goethe all exemplified
the cult of the pilgrim. To his way of thinking, none of these men
understood Jesus and the kingdom of God that He tried to
proclaim—unlike William Blake, Friedrich Schlegel, and Robert
Browning, who had endeavoured to create countermyths that were
not keyed to the individual man. Grønbech speaks in particular
about Browning's *Saul* and even reproduces a part of it in Danish.
There is much other evidence of Grønbech's admiration for William
Blake but this is the only place in his work where Grønbech spoke in
any detail about Robert Browning who, according to the testimony
of members of Grønbech's own family, was Grønbech's favorite
poet. Grønbech's skepticism toward Goethe, which is found
throughout his two volume study of the German writer, here finds
more concentrated expression. Goethe, says Grønbech, was for
modern men what Dante was for the Middle Ages. Faust passed
through events of this world, but the events of this world do not pass
through him; as a consequence Goethe's drama ends in a sphere
above this world and the vision of God that the medieval saints
enjoyed has for Goethe become beauty: "Religion has become
aesthetics," writes Grønbech pejoratively. Grønbech also chides
Goethe for being an old-fashioned spiritual aristocrat, that is, a man
who believed that the proper experiencing of life was open not to
every man but only to the chosen. Grønbech intimates that the path
to democracy that would open life and a paradise on earth to all was
through capitalism. In fact, chapter 5 of *Kampen for en ny sjæl* is
entitled "Capitalism," which Grønbech calls "the genial solution of
practical difficulties connected with the pilgrim's ideal desire for
life."[9] In fact, Grønbech's own attitude toward capitalism as we
generally conceive it must be considered ambivalent, but he felt
that only with the advent of capitalism could the laborer finally
enjoy the fruits of his own labor. Under capitalism one did not work
toward a future life but toward the creation of a stable world in
which life was not merely an exercise for something that was to
come.

Here as elsewhere Grønbech puts questions rather than gives
answers when he is assessing conditions that obtain in the modern
world. He is critical, ironic, and incisive in his observations. Time
and again they possess an epigrammatic quality that makes a lasting
impression upon the mind of the reader who, however, looks in vain
for practical suggestions. Grønbech's generalities, often put in the

form of a question, are striking, without, however, providing the reader with tangibles. Thus, for example, Grønbech suggests: "[I]f I should seriously discover human beings, the world would immediately be changed; most of the painful problems we are struggling with and being crushed by would disappear before realities."[10] Grønbech is immediately defensive in this connection, for he replies rhetorically: "Of course I fully realize that these words will be received by annoyed and presumably disdainful rejection."

III   The Music of Language

A third collection of loosely connected essays is masked behind the title *Sprogets Musik* (*The Music of Language*, 1943). Although Grønbech is concerned with linguistic usage both in general and in imaginative literature in the various parts of this small book, there is no unified argument. The book falls into several parts: the first quarter of the volume is devoted to a discussion about vocabulary, the significance of certain words, and dangers that threaten the effectiveness of language today. There follows a sixty-page discussion of Dickens with casual references to other writers such as Jane Austen, George Eliot, and Balzac. The discussion of Dickens then leads somewhat incongruously into an ambivalent critique of Søren Kierkegaard, which is in turn followed by a series of rather disparate observations about language, popular science, historical writing, French poetry of the nineteenth century, and the contrasting characteristics of prose and poetry.

The point of departure for the argument in the first part of *Sprogets Musik* is a collection of Grønbech's own poems published

Paths). Grønbech had been disappointed at the lack of response to his poetry and the observation of some readers that they did not understand his intent with the verse. He had made a curious suggestion about how the poems should be read, a suggestion that seemed to indicate that they should be chanted according to "their own melody." The lack of understanding for Grønbech's suggestion now made him reflect on the existence of melody and language and specifically the melodic peculiarity intrinsic to a hymn as opposed to a romance. In reality Grønbech was calling attention to the fact that both the substance and the form of an articulated idea or feeling determines its delivery and interpretation. Grønbech here speaks both as a linguist and as a poet. His discussion of certain words in modern Danish reminds us of the discussion of selected vocabulary that was the nucleus of *The Culture of the Teutons*, his first great work. At the same time, Grønbech is personally involved as a poet. He takes the position that there is no real difference between the effective and proper use of words and writing poetry: Grønbech marvels at Dickens' ability to represent on paper the kind of language that we use in everyday intercourse with others, and he doubts whether any other writer in world literature is Dickens' equal on this score. About a third of *Sprogets Musik* is directly or indirectly concerned with Dickens and might well have been published as a separate study rather than as a part of a series of more general observations. It is conceivable that Grønbech may have elected to be unobtrusive in his examination of an English author at a time when the German occupation of Denmark was at a critical stage.

From what has been alluded to before, the reader is aware of Grønbech's aversion to Kierkegaard's religious and philosophical position. Grønbech does not try to make amends with Kierkegaard philosophically, but he recognizes Kierkegaard's geniality and mastery of the Danish language. He calls Kierkegaard's works "a monument to the deification of the individual,"[11] but a few pages later he identifies Kierkegaard's language as "a work of art, which one continues to study with growing admiration."[12] Grønbech goes on to say that Kierkegaard created "an entirely new language, constructed from old theological formulas, and German philosophical jargon but infused with his own unique style." The poetic and creative is the soul of language in all men, high and low, and indeed poetic fruitfulness is often the greatest in people who have not been blessed with too much education and book knowledge."[13] One subheading of the discussion of vocabulary is simply entitled "The Word is a Poem."

Grønbech is a champion of precision and richness in language and is consequently kindly disposed to loan words when they serve a useful purpose. He is highly critical of the movement for linguistic purification in Denmark—and there has been such a movement in Denmark, as in Germany, Norway, Iceland, and certain other countries where a kind of cultural nationalism has been rampant—and calls the purifiers "burglars, who steal our coffee spoons and teaspoons and dessert spoons and soup spoons and marmelade spoons and instead leave one medium sized ladle with the inscription 'can be used to stir the pot and to transfer liquid food to the mouth.' "[14]

Dickens serves Grønbech as a source of examples for the study of human speech—speech in the broadest sense of the term, that is, including gestures and those aspects of communication that more recently have come to be classified under the heading semiotics. Grønbech discusses amusingly the plasticity of body language in Dickens, exemplified by rubbing the nose, cocking the head on one side, or lifting an eyebrow. He runs through Dickens' works and points to the many characters who have their own peculiarities of speech which make them inimitable in imaginative literature. Grønbech finds that Dickens is a true realist since he is able masterfully to reproduce on paper the language and accompanying mannerisms that we employ daily with our fellow men. Because of Dickens' ability to make characters recognizable through the melody of their speech, Grønbech calls Dickens the "greatest dramatist of the nineteenth century."[15]

Somewhat incongruously, the conclusion of Grønbech's remarks about Dickens leads into a critical comment about the church and Puritanism that provides some of the background for the social order of which Dickens was such an incisive if oblique critic. We find Grønbech taking up one of his favorite theses again—that the unity of religion and society, of church and people, ceased in the eighteenth century and that the religious philosophy of Puritanism and Methodism that took the upper hand made the individual all-important. A corollary of this thesis is the rejection of Søren Kierkegaard, who is looked upon as the embodiment of the epidemic religious sickness of the nineteenth and twentieth centuries. Grønbech complains that throughout Kierkegaard's life Kierkegaard did nothing but sit before a mirror and paint a series of self-portraits. "This ideal must necessarily destroy every society."[16] But Kierkegaard was also creative in the realm of language, and Grønbech acknowledges that Kierkegaard created a new language. One can almost say, avers Grønbech, that he gave Zion a court language: he cannot be read without a special glossary.

The remainder of *Sprogets Musik* consists of a series of loosely connected but stimulating observations about language in general, the comprehension of words on the part of a historian, problems of translation, and the interpretation of the past by means of the recreation or renewal of older poetry. Grønbech expressed several prin-

ciples that guided him in his own work. At least three are worth
mentioning here: First, Grønbech stresses that the historian has not
learned a language of the past until he is able to experience the
world as the speakers of the past did. Second, he admits that language can be studied from the standpoint of its form but avers that
comprehension of a language is granted only by cognition with regard to its content. This principle accounts for his standoffish attitude toward all aesthetic criticism. Third, he defends the right to
rework the monuments of the past in the service of the present, "so
that the monuments express something that we feel."[17]

In this part of the book there are numerous other pointed and
epigrammatic remarks which, when taken in the aggregate, grant a
more personal and clearer understanding of Grønbech's private
convictions than do his synthetic and summary works. As a consequence, one can also discern what must be defined as Grønbech's
prejudices. His remarks are not casual and subject to discussion and
revision but suggest rather strong conviction and inflexibility. In the
final chapter of the book, entitled "Prose and Verse," Grønbech
returns to his original argument regarding the melody that the
reader must sense if he is to appreciate poetry. The vast difference
between prose and poetry that exists today Grønbech feels to be a
consequence of a development since the Renaissance and he puts
the blame on the aesthetic requirements that have been established
for poetry and that stress formal content and poetic technique over
emotion. The modern division between prose and poetry he looks
upon as symbolic, as a division into two worlds, the poetic and the
prosaic, which perhaps ideally should be one but are now so different one from the other that events in the poetic world do not correspond to the events of the prosaic world. Grønbech is here suggesting that imaginative literature is not performing the function that it
should and might, for it is divorced from the everyday; poetry has
become a matter of dogma; and criticism has failed to understand
that an appreciation of the melody of literature—a musical quality
that can differ from author to author and not only from language to
language—transcends mere comprehension of content and form.

In the view of the fact that the literature of France was slighted in
Grønbech's book on the *Religious Currents of the Nineteenth Century,* it is of interest to note that he exhibits familiarity with the
best-known French poets of the nineteenth century in *Sprogets
Musik.* In discussing the problem of translation, and notably of

poetry in the last section of *Sprogets Musik,* Grønbech chooses several examples from the French. He employs a sample of successful translation by Johannes Jörgensen—Denmark's leading Catholic writer—of verse by Mallarmé.

Just as Grønbech had clearly defined opinions regarding the English poets—we have learned that his favorite was Browning—so too he expressed his opinions regarding French poets: Verlaine is looked upon as the "greatest of all the masters" because his language is naturally imbued with poetic melody—whereas Victor Hugo's poetry is thought to resemble a huge hurdy-gurdy. In passing, Grønbech also mentions Maurras and Regnier, Baudelaire and Samain. The nature of his judgments is less important than the fact that he harbored understanding and feeling for so many French poets despite the very limited role that French culture and literature seem otherwise to have played in his published works.

IV   *Speaking to a Broader Public*

During the German occupation in World War II, Vilhelm Grønbech's lectures had attracted more and more public attention both within the university and elsewhere. The reason may be that the essential questions of human existence that are the concern of the historian of religion now seemed to be more compelling and less esoteric and academic than in the years of economic pressures and political dissension preceding the conflict. Or the reason may be merely that the course of history had reached a stage where Grønbech's critical and analytical ideas seemed more interesting and more in tune with the times than previously had been the case. Grønbech's popularity continued immediately after the war. He had had large and receptive audiences—but there was a still greater potential audience for his words, spoken or written. At the same time, he felt moved to assume the role of the teacher-provocateur and guide for those of his countrymen who would listen. He therefore took the initiative to establish a periodical that would permit him and others to publish thoughts on issues of the day in a readily accessible form. Although he was not personally very well acquainted with Hal Koch, the socially and politically conscious professor of ecclesiastical history at the University of Copenhagen who also had spoken to a large audience during and after the war while working for relief from the yoke of the German occupation, Grønbech suggested to Koch that the two of them edit a periodical. *Frie*

Ord (Free Words) commenced publication in 1946; in the first issue
there were articles only by the two editors (a fact that caused some
wry comment), but in subsequent issues there were various other
contributors, several of whom had a fairly close relationship to
Grønbech. *Frie Ord* was, however, Grønbech's creation, and he
remained its leading contributor. Although the editors promised
little in a somewhat plaintive foreword, which indicated first and
foremost that *Frie Ord* would differ from other current Danish
periodicals, the journal was an immediate success and within a few
months had six thousand subscribers—an astonishing figure considering the size of the country, the number of other periodicals available, and the rather abstract and thoughtful nature of the articles
that the first numbers of *Frie Ord* carried.

One can only conclude that what Grønbech and Koch had to say
found receptive readers. The two academics' concerns for culture
and their awareness of a postwar cultural crisis were shared by many
of their countrymen who sought articulation and elucidation of the
fundamental problems of the day. Grønbech and Koch addressed
themselves only in a very limited way to what could be identified as
immediate social, political, or economic questions for which arbitrary or pragmatic answers might be given. On the contrary,
they—and Grønbech in particular—put a finger on the pulse of
human existence: the philosophical and religious convictions that
ultimately determined how men acted as individuals and in concert.
Patent, partisan solutions they did not proffer. Grønbech's analyses
are overwhelmingly negative. His persistent irony is sensed
throughout—and one number even contained a short essay by him
on "irony." At a time when it was both easy and popular to reject
Germans and German culture out of hand, while at the same time
elevating everything that was English, Grønbech demonstrated a
cool, analytic mind in a series of articles entitled "The English, the
Germans, and the Rest of us" which spoke harshly of English self-
satisfaction and superficiality as well as recent German brutality and
aggressiveness. What was visible and easy to condemn, one concluded from Grønbech's argument, was really an effect, whereas
a flawed basic assumption—philosophical and religious com-
promise—was a cause. As a consequence, G. B. Shaw and H. G.
Wells fared no better than Nietzsche, when viewed through a
National Socialist prism, or the Swedish manipulator Ivar Kreuger.

Time and again Grønbech turned to the New Testament for an

analogical argument: the parables of Jesus and the questions put by the Messiah he found valid and applicable in addressing his contemporaries. One might wonder whether Grønbech was some kind of cryptomissionary for the established faith—a traditional believer, a good Lutheran who hitherto had hid his conservative beliefs behind a veil of imagery and irony—but evidence from all his other works negates such a supposition. He was, rather, using imagery that, because of its associations in a Christian, Lutheran country, would not miss fire. Perhaps, too, he was again assuming the role of the believer in order to make his point as he had done so many times previously in earlier writings.

There is no doubt that Grønbech was purveying a message in *Frie Ord*, despite the multiplicity of matters about which he expressed himself. He was once more stressing the interrelationship of the individual and an organized society—but a society that was based on metaphysical belief rather than on an arbitrary social order or political system. The mere title, "Who is my Neighbor," of one series of articles is a striking formulation suggesting the need for the individual to realize his spiritual interdependence on his fellow man. A poignant statement is the brief essay, "What Shall I Do?"[18] "Yes," says Grønbech, "what shall we do to be glad and happy?"— repeating a recurrent question but a question that has been put more insistently in the twentieth century than before, since the twentieth century (and indeed modern time as Grønbech would delimit it: since the victory of rationalism at the end of the eighteenth century) does not look upon earthly existence as a mere prelude to a future life but essentially as life's alpha and omega. Grønbech states very simply that something has gone wrong with our culture. The fantasy of progress has misled man, while the natural and physical scientist, who so optimistically had been expected to solve all our problems, is observed himself to be disappointed and dissatisfied. The creation of dreadful and efficient new weapons of war are sufficient reason to undertake a reassessment and revaluation of our practical assumptions and priorities. It is easy enough to join in the chorus of voices that complain of the dominance of a machine culture, Grønbech points out, but such complaints seem to lead only to resignation. They do not bring about a solution. Grønbech derives a certain amount of satisfaction from noting that an awareness of the cultural crisis of which he had been speaking for thirty years finally had penetrated the consciousness of the average man. There are observers who presume that the flaw lies somewhere within the machine; if the machine can be repaired, then the problems facing us may be solved. Not so, says Grønbech. The flaw is that we have unreservedly put our faith in the sciences. The sciences have become our abstract religion, but they are brittle constructs. Since the machine is purely man-made, it cannot fulfill the metaphysical needs of its maker.

Once more Grønbech elects to use the parables of Jesus to project his argument; the surprising leap from the twentieth century into the disputes of Jesus with the Talmudic scholars of the first century "seemed to me suitable," said Grønbech, "more suitable than anything else I could think of to solve the dilemma upon which we are now impaled."[19] Jesus was questioning a system of knowledge—which could be called either a science or a religion—of the time, but He brought no practical panacea for the world's ills, for the only solution lies in the self-recognition of the individual's own flaws and of his obligation to his fellow man. Grønbech notes, almost with a sigh, that this message from the first century probably will be shrugged off as impractical and utopian, and as a reactionary effort to block progress. It is not a matter of living according to a set of ideals, concludes Grønbech, but of determining whether the ideals are properly conceived. Is the basis upon which our ideals rest sufficiently broad—or "so narrow that the structure of culture, despite its magnificent façade, becomes a prison rather than a home?"[20]

One of the series of articles published in *Frie Ord*, entitled "Dostoevski and his Russia," is as much a reflection of the position of Russia within European culture as it is a study of the Russian novelist. The popular quality of the lengthy essay on Dostoevski is suggested by the fact that Grønbech read Dostoevski only in Danish translation, whereas in all his other works he had worked with the original texts (while not eschewing the use of translations that were available). Grønbech does discuss some of Dostoevski's novels, but the basic ideas that inform them and the philosophical assumptions upon which they rest are of much greater interest to him than the content and form of the narrative. The articles—which after Grønbech's death were collected and published in book form—were not meant primarily as a contribution to literary history but rather to an understanding of the difference between the Russian attitude toward life and the West European attitude, and to the recognition of

what can be called Russia's cultural mission. Like some recent critics, Grønbech early saw the interrelationship between the
nineteenth-century novelist and the twentieth-century new order in
Russia. For him Dostoevski was also a harbinger of what was to
come in Eastern Europe. Dostoevski was as different from the
novelists of the West as Russian society after the revolution is different from Western European society. But Dostoevski had the function as well of mediating the metaphysical assumptions, the "Russian soul," in the West.

Without in any way entering into political debate, Grønbech intimates in this book, with Dostoevski as the point of departure, that
the Soviet Union seems to have been able to create a new faith and
to constitute a vast new congregation of believers. While Grønbech
does not mention the possibility of the equation of Communism
with religion, the conclusion is inescapable that a new, doctrinary
faith that millions have accepted either out of conviction or indoctri-
nation, is indeed a religion. Grønbech did not indicate the Soviet
Union's new faith and the political structure that is intertwined with
that faith is exportable, but he did declare that the West must learn
to understand the outward changes that had come about in Russia in
the twentieth century and to accept this new permutation of the
Russian soul if peaceful coexistence was to obtain. Just as the European Christian errs when he would interfere with the realistic unity
of a distant religion, so too, Grønbech intimates, does the European
politician err when he would interfere with the functional unity of
Soviet Communism. To understand Grønbech's perspicacity and
courage, one should bear in mind that he was writing in 1947.

CHAPTER 9

Grønbech's Idiom

THAT the impact of poets and thinkers can be explained not simply on the basis of what they say but because of the way in which they say it is a truism; nevertheless, the observation is strikingly applicable in the case of Vilhelm Grønbech. At times he is able to express himself with great precision and at other times in such a wilfully imprecise way that the reader is forced to reflect or even to grope his way along some new path. Grønbech's vocabulary transects the maze of human experience.

If Grønbech himself had not been such a master of language, the impact of much of his work would have been considerably lessened and his position in Danish cultural history would have been different. He was a great rhetorician, but not in a pejorative sense: he had received a rigorous classical schooling and was aware of the principles of style. He was familiar with the figures of speech and could use them effectively. He was expert with forceful imagery; he could manipulate language for his own purposes without merely being swept along by a current of impressive words of his own creation; and he was not afraid to coin original phrases or to employ little-used or archaic terms if they conveyed with precision what he might want to say.

The peculiar quality of Grønbech's work is explicable only by considering the compelling metaphorical idiom, the frequent use of hyperbole, and the ubiquitous tendency to speak with the conviction of the convinced. Over and over again Grønbech created images and phrases that ingratiate themselves in the mind of his reader. Over and over again he enunciated generalities that, when examined strictly from a logical standpoint, may be considered questionable, but that nevertheless possessed such an element of truth—be it but a brilliant half truth—that the reader was unwilling to stop and debate with Grønbech and was, rather, impelled to read on, to see how Grønbech's argument develops. Two remarkable examples of this kind of style are the first paragraph of *Religious Currents of the Nineteenth Century* (1922)[1] (cf. p. 43, *supra*), and several sentences from the beginning of his essay "On Reading," which also originally appeared in 1922 (and was republished in 1930 in the collection *Kampen om mennesket*, "The Struggle for the Human Being"):

To this very day, reading and writing are a sacred art; books open the way to bind and loose souls; and because the alphabet possesses such powers, we do our best to initiate as many as possible into the secrets of the symbols. . . . The principal task of modern culture is to increase the desire to read and to place in people's hands the means to engender a love of the printed word. . . . Now more than ever before reading is a sacred art, for the way from the individual to the surrounding world is only through the book.[2]

Here are some of Grønbech's most incisive observations, formulated in a rhythmic, alliterative, and elevated prose.

There are examples of unusual and complex metaphors in Grønbech's works. Consider a brief passage in the volume on Indian mysticism from the year 1925, where he speaks of "that sort of fine tones which are so terribly hard to sing purely but just those kinds of tone often create the music of speculative theology."[3] At times one even finds a use of metaphor with erotic overtones in Grønbech, as in the statement "God and the soul impinge more and more excitedly upon one another and inflict mutually deep wounds; each tears off its veil; there is a flashing and sparkling from the one end to the other until both turn into flames after being united."[4]

Not infrequently he uses repetition, variation, and parallel dramatically in order to increase the effect of what he has to say. In *Jesus*, one can read a passage that combines all three devices: "This world with its complex of commandments and forms, with its kingdoms where men rule one another, with its courts where they play tug-of-war in the name of justice, with its significance for the family and its devils and sicknesses."[5]

Grønbech's independence of spirit and at the same time the seriousness of his sense of mission is suggested by a quotation from his essay on Herder contained in the fourth volume of the series devoted to mystics: "If a man has something serious on his mind he has to use the language in his own way, and the only connection he has with the dictionary is that he provides lexicographers with something to do in that they must revise their work."[6]

Since none of Vilhelm Grønbech's manuscripts are known to exist and since very few of his letters are preserved or accessible, it is difficult to speak authoritatively about the genesis of what he wrote. Several members of his family are, however, in agreement in their testimony that he rewrote his books several times prior to publication—a minimum of four times would be no exaggeration according to statements by those who knew him. It has also been said by persons who were close to Grønbech that his first wife was, at least at times, of great assistance to him in the rewriting process, but just what her contribution was cannot be determined.

Perhaps because he tended to rewrite so much, there is a noticeable paucity of references to sources and secondary works in many of his publications. There is no doubt about his familiarity with the sources, and one would presume that he at least in the first round had quoted directly and perhaps made some notation of the sources of quotations. In the final version of many of his works, such bibliographical references are often lacking and may be presumed simply to have fallen by the wayside. To be sure, internal evidence suggests that Grønbech frequently relied on his memory, and when he was doing so, he did not employ quotation marks to suggest direct quotation. In fact, he was not given to using quotation marks at all. As has been noted above several times, it is characteristic of his style that one often has difficulty in distinguishing between Grønbech and the subject about whom he is writing.

In this connection, attention may be called to an undated essay by Grønbech first published in the Danish periodical *Perspektiv* seven years after his death. One finds here an enlightening autobiographical observation: "My favorite reading was biographies and letters of thinkers, scientists, poets, moralists, physicians, theologians, and ordinary folk. I wasn't satisfied with knowing simply what a human being thought and how he thought but why he had to think the way he did. In this way I could myself experience him"[7] Much earlier— in 1916, in an article about Edvard Lehmann (his predecessor at the University of Copenhagen)—Grønbech had defined the function of the historian of religion as the ability to identify himself with other mortals who thought differently from him and to partake in their happiness and sorrow. Grønbech followed his own advice.

An especially good example of this method is to be found in

Grønbech's essay on Heraclitus contributed to the yearbook of the academy of sciences in Lund, Sweden, in 1929.[8] Grønbech interprets the fragments of Heraclitus without giving references to sources. Although he speaks for Heraclitus, he is also expressing his own ideas which he interweaves with those of Heraclitus, so that it is nearly impossible to distinguish Grønbech from Heraclitus. Furthermore, Grønbech hyperbolizes and synthesizes freely on the basis not only of the preserved evidence but also of his own assumptions, insofar as he interprets Heraclitus to be both a mystic and a champion of the aristocratic order. Grønbech writes as if he were quite in accord with Heraclitus; he is the master explicator rather than the critic. It is further apparent that, in this particular case, Grønbech is trying to construct a system or achieve some unity out of the fragments of Heraclitus—a task that combines subjectivity and insight.

Grønbech made the same point in a different way in his study of Saint Theresa where he wrote: "The function of the historian is to find the human being behind the pose, and the requisite for a scholar to reach his goal is that he learn the language that his heroes speak."[9] That is, the historian should familiarize himself thoroughly with the primary sources—in this case everything that Theresa had written. Then one should describe the various aspects of the subject by paraphrasing words and ideas in such a way that they can be identified with the subject. That means, in this case, Grønbech's identifying himself with Theresa so that the reader is scarcely able to distinguish between Theresa and her spokesman Grønbech. In numerous places in the book on Theresa, Grønbech writes as if he were a believer; if one knew less about Grønbech one would assume that he must indeed have been a co-religionist to be able to portray Theresa the way he did.

Grønbech was skeptical of the dominant pragmatic method of historiography—and he found in Plutarch an ironic definition of the writing of history to the effect that historiography should not consist of telling what has happened, for that is nothing but an unending tiresome series of seductions of women, the plotting of slaves, the defamation of friends, the mixing of poison, jealousy, hatred, the ruin of lineages, and the fall of princes.[10] In his essay on John Donne Grønbech wrote more pointedly: "The historical and psychological method consists of overcoming human nature by a sorting process. We divide a man up, construct periods in his life, and we create an interesting connection within him by introducing an interpretation. In so doing we have the advantage of avoiding having to confront that difficult something which is called the human soul. . . ."11 Grønbech's goal was to penetrate to the soul and to be able to describe what he had found.

Since one tends to praise those traits in another person's character that one not only admires but hopes one possesses, it is of particular interest to examine Grønbech's memorial to the Danish philosopher Harald Høffding, which he delivered at a meeting of the Danish Academy of Sciences in December 1931. Some of the phrases in the very first paragraph of Grønbech's address provide a striking parallel to any description of Grønbech. Høffding's works, Grønbech began, "were an imposing monument over an active life," and "the books that he had written were not only a reminder of a scholar's tireless zeal, but a monument over a human being's unbroken struggle in order to live in spirit and in truth." He went on to state that the "endless pages gave witness of a soul that not only had struggled but also had suffered in order to find itself, to become a human being in the highest sense of the word."12

Grønbech observed that Høffding had been born into the dilemma of the nineteenth century—the contrast between faith and knowledge—and that his research had begun as a kind of monologue in order to achieve clarity with himself. Høffding's works Grønbech found to bear a personal stamp and his research to have originated from the innermost drive of his own personality. All these remarks are applicable to Vilhelm Grønbech himself. The figure of Høffding and the ideas associated with him were so titillating to Grønbech that the necrology has an unusual breadth. Numerous ideas that informed Grønbech's *Religious Currents of the Nineteenth Century* are here again identifiable, and the reader learns of Grønbech's convictions as much as Høffding's. An example is found where Grønbech speaks his piece about Kierkegaard, and says that Kierkegaard "had robbed religion of all realities and all content, so that nothing was left but the thorns."13 Grønbech admitted a few pages later that Høffding's own words about Kierkegaard had a rather different slant. The treatment of Kierkegaard here suggests what can be supported by other evidence, namely that Grønbech himself had experienced a confrontation with Kierkegaard's works, had received impulses from Kierkegaard, but had finally rejected him. Grønbech noted that Høffding said that Kierkegaard had helped him find the center of his own personality; if there is any truth in this statement, it may also be applicable to Grønbech.

In view of Grønbech's predilection for a metaphoric style, one of the sentences in the necrology over Høffding is noteworthy: "All answers to the greatest problems of life which transcend the last hypotheses of science can have but a poetic character, which does not hinder their having a religious meaning as the most living expressions that can be found to describe the relationship we experience between value and actuality."[14]

Particularly striking in the necrology of Høffding is the statement that "Høffding always sought synthesis but it was always a certain harmony which he expected—and found."[15] No two concepts could be more essential to a description of Grønbech's work than synthesis and harmony; Grønbech was unsurpassed as a synthesist of his time and harmony was ever his watchword.

Notable too are the remarks that Grønbech makes about Høffding's relationship to Nietzsche. We know that Grønbech was aware of Nietzsche and that there are not a few parallels that may be drawn between the German and the Danish thinkers. In fact, according to Grønbech's widow, Honorine Hermelin Grønbech, a study of Nietzsche was on Grønbech's agenda at his death in 1948. Grønbech spoke of Høffding's confrontation with Nietzsche as something of an earthquake where his loyalty to the past and his evident humanism found their most admirable expression. Whereas Høffding had at first been repelled by Nietzsche, he gained understanding for the German philosopher's ethics, without, however, understanding the danger to the faith of the humanist implicit in Nietzsche's ideal. We glimpse Grønbech's own evaluation of Nietzsche in the words "this German enthusiast who could not be made to mesh with Høffding's ideal of the humane."[16] It is apparent, therefore, that, while Grønbech recognized Nietzsche's brilliance and the stimulus that could be derived from him, he could not accept him. Grønbech and Nietzsche shared numerous convictions and addressed themselves to similar questions, but both their points of origin and their goals were at odds. Their common characteristic was a command of the word and the inspiration that their stylistic dexterity and genius evoked in their readers.

CHAPTER 10

Grønbech: Mentor and Image

IN his last years Grønbech had permeated several levels or circles of intellectual life in Denmark. This is evidenced first by the increased dissemination of his works in book form; second, by the widespread interest in the periodical *Frie Ord*—which Grønbech's co-editor Hal Koch characterized as wholly Grønbech's creation; and third, by the internal evidence demonstrable in the two leading post-World War II critical journals of Denmark: forthrightly and dramatically in *Heretica,* and less directly in *Vindrosen (The Compass).* It has often been said that Grønbech was the inspiration for the founding of *Heretica*—although he was not its founder and indeed not associated in any formal way with that intellectual journal, which is to some extent to parallel to *Frie Ord.* Grønbech must, however, be considered to be the archheretic without whose stimulus the journal would not have taken form. At Grønbech's death in 1948, the third issue of *Heretica* included three memorials by writers who were major figures of the *Heretica* group: Ole Wivel, the journal's publisher; Thorkild Bjørnvig, poet and an editor of *Heretica;* and Martin A. Hansen, a leading Danish novelist and cultural critic. Bjørnvig's article about Grønbech was entitled simply "The Heretic." Grønbech's association with *Heretica*—a journal that came to be looked upon as the rallying point for a new literary orientation in postwar Denmark—has been examined in a special study by Birgit Helene Hansen (1970). *Heretica* printed a total of five contributions by Grønbech, two of them shortened versions of public lectures that Grønbech had given in 1931 and 1947 respectively—"Religion" and "Angst." In the early *Vindrosen,* which to a certain degree is a successor to *Heretica,* one senses an awareness of Grønbech's thinking, without that journal's having published any contribution by or about Grønbech. Of the many writers who felt the impact of Grønbech, Martin A. Hansen was the

140

most important. Several of his works do much to try to create a perfect reality. Like Grønbech—and frequently quoting Grønbech—he pointed to the lost harmony of medieval Christianity, notably in his highly individual work with the symbolic title *Orm og Tyr (Serpent and Ox,* 1952).

Numerous new editions of Grønbech's works were published in the 1950s and 1960s, but with the passing of time he became both less controversial and less the authority to be evoked in discussions of current, contemporary problems, and more a historical figure. Still, no canonical profile of Grønbech has emerged, although some historical study of his work has been undertaken. The number of articles about Grønbech published in his lifetime and shortly after his death is legion; there was then a seed of the polemical sown only by the mention of his name. Gradually, certain of his works seem to have assumed more lasting importance than others, but it is still perplexing to make an highly selective, intelligent division among his interpretive works into those items that deserve serious consideration and those that are of lesser importance. The difficulty of making such a decision is demonstrated in the most recent (1974) study of Grønbech, a lengthy Danish work in two volumes by Ejvind Riisgaard, who undertakes to describe the entire *œuvre* with impartiality but admiration and, especially, with an eye to recurrent themes.

Incidentally, Riisgaard's book, like many articles and reviews that previously were published pertaining to Grønbech, is renewed evidence of the overweening tendency of critics to quote or to paraphrase Grønbech when trying to explain his work. Riisgaard, like every other critical reader of Grønbech, has been struck continually by passages that are worthy of mediating to others through quotation or paraphrase. The moral that can be drawn from this state of affairs is simple: the critic is in essence urging the reader to make firsthand acquaintance with a stimulating thinker, an incisive synthesist, an original mind, and a brilliant rhetorician.

Through the publication of several posthumous works, the image of a viable Grønbech was upheld for several years after his death. The lectures he had given at Borup's College in Copenhagen in 1943, and which had been taken down in shorthand by one of his hearers, have been mentioned above in connection with the discussion of *Hellas.* This work, entitled *The Light from the Acropolis,* was a readily accessible distillation of much of the substance contained in the more demanding series of volumes on *Hellas*. *Hellas*, too, had a direct supplement in the fifth, posthumously published volume that contained, in addition to indices to the first four volumes, additional chapters on the festivals of the peasants—it would be more accurate to say franklins—and on the gods. Further, a fragmentary study of Philo Judea was edited by Grønbech's former student Povl Johannes Jensen (later professor of classics in the University of Copenhagen) as *Philon* (1949). It supplemented the work on Hellenism.

The one posthumous work that was not merely an addition to an earlier work or the printing of previously unpublished lectures was *Livet er et fund* (*Life is a Discovery*, 1951). Grønbech had been engaged with the book at his death; it was incomplete and not as yet organized as he might ultimately have done it. Title and subtitle ("A book about humor and tragedy") do not stem from his pen and are rather inaccurate designations. The book is nevertheless one of Grønbech's most accessible and makes entertaining and stimulating reading. It consists of a series of literary essays that might well first have been published in the periodical *Frie Ord* if Grønbech had lived. Grønbech's first concern here is with humor—or rather the lack of humor from which the West has suffered since the Reformation—but the substance of the book really consists of repetitions and echos of the *leitmotifs* from Grønbech's previous work: the lot of modern man isolated from the society in which he lives; the cultivation of the single soul à la Kierkegaard with a disregard for the need of participation in a community; the want of a true religion that can permeate every phase of life; the danger of aestheticism that is not anchored in a philosophical conviction; and, finally, the need for myth—these are major concerns that have been seen in various earlier books and articles by Grønbech. In this final work, however, Grønbech is not a gloomy prophet. Despite the repetition of his negative observations about modern man, Grønbech is on the one hand convinced of the possibility for improvement (but not perfection) of the state of the human being, on the other hand appreciative of the delightfully human quality of humor and of the insights that humor furnishes into human character while at the same time it relieves and entertains a mind that has been under tension or stress. There is an interrelationship with Grønbech's earlier book *The Language of Music*: Dickens again becomes for Grønbech the able and incomparable creator of entertaining characters and situations.

Between Grønbech's death in April 1948 and the year 1957, several volumes were issued that were chiefly reprints of various contributions from *Frie Ord*, now in collected form rather than as a sequence of essays spread through several issues of that periodical. The first of these collections (1948) comprised the essays that had evoked Dostoevski's name. Another, shorter series of essays, entitled *Minstrels and Other People*, was issued, ostensibly privately, the next year. The two above-mentioned lectures, "Religion" (1931) and "Angst" (1947), first printed in *Heretica* in 1951, were issued as a small separate volume in 1951. A lecture that Grønbech once held at the Copenhagen students' union on "Students and schoolboys" appeared separately in 1956. The following year several series of essays from *Frie Ord*, including the address to the Copenhagen students, were issued in book form as *Atombomben og andre essays*. With this item, the long series of published works by Grønbech, which had begun fifty-five years earlier, came to an end. Grønbech had moved from a narrowly defined discipline of philology through the history of religion and the history of culture, to achieve eminence as an outstanding historian of religion and culture, and finally to become a well-known and prestigious cultural figure whose pronouncements on a variety of subjects won the attention of a general audience.

One might have expected the publication of Grønbech's letters and possibly other papers in the intervening years, but Grønbech had admonished members of his family and co-workers that his papers should be destroyed. Only a handful of letters has been made public. There is no shortcut to knowing Grønbech: his work is his life. Beyond that, Grønbech's personal life, like that of most university professors and scholars, is uninteresting.

CHAPTER 11

Conclusion

G RØNBECH was important to his own time and speaks to us still today because he was able to identify and explain the spiritual needs of modern man. While it may be objected that he was only an analyst and diagnostician, analysis and diagnosis are essential to any cure—that is, to positive and creative future development. It has been said more than once that Grønbech's work was in essence a summing up, a settling of accounts. Thirty years ago when Grønbech's influence on thought in the folk-high-school circles of Denmark was particularly evident, the head of the Askov Folk High School, J. Th. Arnfred, used the term *opgør*—that is, a settling of accounts—to describe Grønbech's work, and this same term appears again in the subtitle of the most recent Danish study of Grønbech, the two-volume work by Ejvind Riisgaard. In an article in the Danish newspaper *Politiken*, Peter P. Rohde had written with somewhat greater precision, "Grønbech's works can be viewed as one gigantic effort to determine what is required of society that human beings may live happily in it . . . and why men in society in our own times have been so divided, isolated, and unhappy."[1] Men, many men, perhaps most men of the twentieth century have felt themselves spiritually at loose ends, without being able to describe their symptoms or know what it was that made them restless and dissatisfied. What was ineffable for most, Grønbech was able to put into words—not simply denotative terms, but imaginative phraseology that stimulated men's minds to new thought and engendered in them new hope. That is, Grønbech was functioning both as a poet and a thinker, sometimes indeed very nearly as a priest, and yet he had no patent set of beliefs to offer, no confession to which men should subscribe, and no organization with which they might affiliate. In order to find their way out of chaos and the morass of contemporary life, they required an understanding of their own

144

situation, new imagery, and a restatement of metaphysical values. This Grønbech would give them. Various critics have remarked that Vilhelm Grønbech was a modern prophet, but the term is misleading. Insofar as he provides an explanation of existence that brings with it a spiritual awakening, he can perhaps loosely be called a prophet, but he had no doctrine to which one can take recourse in all situations and no blueprint of the future.

Those currents of thought that were basic in any culture were for Grønbech identifiable as religious currents. The beliefs that make men act as they do constitute their religion, whether or not there is a formal ecclesiastical organization involved. In this sense Grønbech speaks of the religious currents of the nineteenth century (as he does in his book by that title) and means only in part organized religion and in part such disparate phenomena as the works of Goethe, the theories of Darwin, and the belief in science and technology as the salvation of man. By the same token, those figures of the past who have given a different direction to men's minds and who have exerted a lasting effect upon society can be subsumed under religion. Thus Goethe and Herder can be considered within the context of late eighteenth and early nineteenth-century religion. To be sure, Herder was himself a clergyman, but the influential ideas that emanated from Herder seemed to have no connection with his theological training or practice. And no one would associate Goethe with organized religion, despite his having employed the symbols of the Christian church in certain places in his works. Similarly, one might wonder why Wordsworth and Blake could attract Grønbech or why he could devote so much attention to the works of the German writer Friedrich Schlegel. In fact, Grønbech made no effort to treat these three men as religious figures; he was attracted to them because of the originality of their convictions and the prophetic quality of their thought. Their ideas were going to find resonance and acceptance in the future; in their lives and works they are in part helping mold the future.

As a historian of religion, Grønbech was convinced of the importance of religion, and probably for this reason he never broke with the established Lutheran church into which he was born. Nor did he try to refine it or hold out any hope that some new reformation would bring men who had experienced chaos back into the fold as believers. Time and again, he insisted that men's greatest need was a new myth, without, however, being able to explain what the new myth should be, at least not in the terms of traditional religion. Even though he saw strong new faiths established and attracting believers who were full of optimism, these new faiths—as forceful and influential as they might be—were unlike the religions of the past, for they did not provide complete satisfaction, since they could not fill out the perimeter of man's existence: in the nineteenth century, the doctrine of evolution; in the twentieth, the labor movement and the women's movement.

Grønbech repeatedly pointed out the need for myth. By myth he meant a metaphysical construct, a system of belief shared by a community of believers, and a means to answer some of the recurrent problems of human existence. In *The Culture of the Teutons*, he described the myth that provided a unity of life in Germanic antiquity: certain basic concepts were shared by all members of society; these concepts were not questioned—in fact, one was scarcely rationally aware of their existence. The existence of supernatural forces was taken for granted and a system of relationships to these supernatural forces was evolved. The relationship of man to man and man to gods was co-determined if not predetermined by the unquestioned basic assumptions of existence. Such a situation was prerequisite for the existence of harmony.

Grønbech saw an analogous situation in the religion of classical Greece. The basic arguments that informed *The Culture of the Teutons* are found again in his five-volume study *Hellas*. Germanic antiquity had had its myth that allowed the souls of men to partake of harmony; Hellas had had its comparable myth. Christianity had subsequently provided a new formulation and a new myth and had attracted a community of believers who accepted more refined or simpler tenets. Under scrutiny, any myth tends to break down, however. As more and more questions pertaining to the unknown were subjected to rational analysis in modern times, the hold of the new myth was lessened, with the subsequent dissolution of harmony.

A new myth means a new reality, but the reality must have its basis in actuality. Actuality, Grønbech had said in *Religious Currents of the Nineteenth Century*, can not be outwitted.[2] He pointed out further that the Christian church of the nineteenth century lagged behind because "It defended the religion of the Renaissance which no longer conformed to actuality."[3]

He who would create a religion or he who would create some-
in 1941 under the title *Solen har mange veje (The Sun Has Many*

thing in which men can believe must be able to make use of myth. Grundtvig was such a person in nineteenth-century Denmark and Grønbech could therefore express admiration for him, although Grundtvig was, as it were, born a millenium too late to be the creator of a religion. He lived at a time when, in Grønbech's words, science had become so dry and simplified that it no longer can fill out a myth. Grundtvig was nevertheless in Grønbech's opinion the greatest man in Danish intellectual history (as he indicated in an article on Edward Lehmann in a Copenhagen newspaper in 1930).[4]

Grønbech was also attracted to William Blake and Friedrich Schlegel, who, he felt, were creating new myths at about the same time in England and Germany respectively. Blake and Schlegel presented mankind with a new possibility; but they were really prophets crying in the wilderness despite their understanding that man needed a new myth and their ability to provide such a myth. Their relative lack of success may perhaps be ascribed to their use of poetic form, for modern man prefers prose to poetry, and the conquering genre of the last two hundred years in European literature has been the novel. Perhaps for this very reason, Grønbech felt moved to write two novels himself, one, *Sejersen fra Variager,* which dealt with the life of the common people on the island of Bornholm—a book that is said to have been written during World War I,[5] but not published until 1940—and *Madonna og gøgleren* (*Madonna and the Juggler,* 1946), a rather loquacious and anecdotal narrative with lyrical intercalations.

Remarkable about Grønbech was his unwillingness to go along with à la mode explanations of human actions. Whereas most of Europe was impressed one way or another by the work of Sigmund Freud, Grønbech rejected it in its totality as overemphasizing a single facet of human life and representing only a sort of prurient curiosity. His denunciation of Freudian psychology—although it was unilateral from the standpoint of any fruitful discussion—does indicate his familiarity with that modern discipline.

Although he expressed himself negatively about Freud, he never wrote about Karl Marx. In the abstract, however, he did recognize the quality of the common shared belief among Communists. Grønbech was never politically active and what political party he might have supported or what program he might have cast a vote for is a matter of conjecture. He was probably as nonpolitical as a thinking person could be in Denmark in the twentieth century. While he could not accept its tenets, Grønbech intimated later in life that Marxism also offered a new myth to those who would believe—an idea that is shared by many other critics, some of whom identify Marxism as a new religion. Grønbech never used the term religion about Marxism in the little that he had to say about it, presumably because Marxism is quite anthropocentric, whereas traditional religion is also concerned with the forces of nature plus an element of the unknown and a sympathetic understanding of the past and relationship to it. It is not possible to be a Marxist mystic.

We have the testimony of some of his students and hearers that he could expound on the atonic thery as well as on the dramas of Euripides. One of Grønbech's students, Leo Buchardt, has stated that Grønbech felt Einstein had seen in the world of nature what he himself had seen in his studies of religion—that is, that reality was relative. Grønbech was of the opinion that Einstein had pointed out a new path for the natural sciences to take, a path that would lead to the recognition of complexity of existence comparable to the metaphysical concept of multiple reality.

Grønbech's cognizance of those currents and movements of the twentieth century which are easily recognized and quickly identified does not enable us to categorize him as anything but an intelligent and alert individual. The fact is that he did not actively engage himself with such currents, for—judged from an objective philosophical standpoint—they are only superficial phenomena. In our examination of Grønbech's work we have seen that he was constantly probing beneath the surface of human experience. While he expressed himself about contemporaries and current events upon numerous occasions, generally speaking he maintained a historical point of view and was always attempting the recognition and analysis of the basic concepts which inform a system of principles, a metaphysical construct, a philosophy, a religion.

He was a thinker. His study was his world. He felt secure in his judgments when they could be based on an intimate knowledge of written evidence. Only relatively later in life did he venture into the realm of the folk-high-school mass meeting and public discussion. Even then he was not willing to brook contradiction generated by opinion rather than fact and he was impatient with the triviality of small talk. His inflexibility derived in part from the strength of convictions that had been slowly, carefully, and thoroughly formulated, but in part also because he despised writers and speakers whose primary aim was to attract attention to themselves rather than to serve the truth as they saw it.

It is, of course, unsatisfactory simply to say that Grønbech was a thinker, for the term is imprecise, although positive in connotation. Yet any other classification must be burdened with reservations: He was a philologist by training and his profound knowledge of languages provided a basis for much of his research; yet he did not function as a linguist after his first two academic publications. He was a historian of religion by profession for thirty years; but many of his publications seem to lie beyond the pale of any traditional religious studies and to be devoted as much to general cultural phenomena as to organized religion. He was a philosopher in that he propounded basic beliefs and the need for a system of ethics that could be shared by a large community of human beings; but he did not himself work out any systematic philosophy. He was a critic of literature; but paid next to no attention to many of the formal facets of imaginative writing that seem to most critics to be essential to evaluation. He was himself a poet; but his command of language in his studies of past cultures and religions had a far greater impact than his own poetry and novels. Not without good reason he has also been called a mystic and a prophet; yet his affiliation with mysticism was short-lived and his study of several mystics are as much exposés as interpretations. And while he did proclaim truths like a prophet by means of striking imagery and by the articulation of modern man's need for a faith, he did not prophesy what would come about and foresaw neither a golden age nor a holocaust.

There is nevertheless one term which is quite valid when applied to Grønbech: he was a synthesist. In the chaotic evidence of the past, he could discern patterns. From disparate testimonies, he was able to derive valid syntheses and thus to open the eyes of his readers and hearers to the essential qualities of ideas, events, and peoples of the past and at the same time to insinuate the existence of comparable patterns and qualities in the present. His keenly analytical mind and his rhetorical facility made an indelible impression on his students and on his hearers during his lifetime. His written analyses and syntheses have been sources of stimulus, inspiration—and sometimes irritation—for thousands of readers. They should remain so for future readers, for little that he wrote has suffered the erosion wrought by time.

Notes and References

Chapter Two

1. *The Culture of the Teutons* (London, 1931), I, 56. All quotations are given from the English version of this work rather than in translation from the original Danish.
2. Ibid., II, 217.
3. Ibid., II, 270.
4. Ibid., I, 14.
5. Ibid., III, 73.
6. *Sprogets Musik* (Copenhagen, 1956), p. 156.
7. *Kristus* (Copenhagen, 1941), p. 106.
8. *Kampen for en ny sjæl* (Copenhagen, 1946), p. 120.
9. *The Culture of the Teutons*, I, 22.
10. *Hellenismen* (Copenhagen, 1939), II, 224.
11. *Mystikere i Europa og Indien* IV (Copenhagen, 1934), 180.
12. *Kristus*, p. 118.
13. *Kampen om mennesket* (Copenhagen and Oslo, 1930), p. 58.

Chapter Three

1. The English title is of the translation originally published by the University of Kansas Press, 1964; repr. (paperback) by Southern Illinois University Press, 1973, Pagination and quotations are from the English translation.
2. *Hellenismen*, I, 203.
3. *Religious Currents in the Nineteenth Century*, 1922, p. 45.
4. Ibid., p. 16.
5. Ibid., p. 96.
6. Ibid., p. 95.
7. Ibid., p. 62.
8. Ibid., p. 97.
9. Ibid., p. 98.
10. Ibid., p. 78.
11. Ibid.
12. Ibid., p. 79.

13. Ibid., p. 81.
14. Ibid., p. 100.
15. Ibid., p. 85.
16. Ibid., p. 87.
17. Ibid., p. 88.
18. Ibid., p. 134.
19. Ibid., p. 138.
20. Ibid., p. 140.
21. Ibid., p. 150.
22. Ibid.
23. Ibid., p. 164.
24. Ibid., p. 175.
25. Ibid., p. 160.
26. Ibid., p. 156.
27. Ibid., p. 25.
28. Ibid., p. 20.

Chapter Four

1. *Mystikere i Europa og Indien* (Copenhagen, vol. I, 1925; II & III, 1932; IV, 1934), IV, 221.
2. *Mystik og Mystikere*, ed. Vilhelm Grønbech and Aage Marcus (Copenhagen, 1930), p. 11.
3. *Religionsskiftet i Norden* (Copenhagen & Kristiania, 1913), p. 60.
4. *Mystikere* I (Copenhagen, 1925), p. 12.
5. Ibid., p. 145.
6. "Heraklit" in *Vetenskaps-Societeten i Lund. Årsbok*, 1929, p. 22.
7. Ibid., p. 32, 33.
8. *Mystikere* II, 63.
9. Ibid., p. 206.
10. Review in *Berlingske Tidende* 24 March 1933.
11. *Mystikere* III, 329.
12. Ibid., p. 65.
13. Ibid., p. 312.
14. Ibid., p. 313.
15. Ibid., p. 325 f.
16. *Religious Currents*, p. 53.
17. Ibid., p. 55.
18. Ibid., p. 61.
19. Ibid., p. 62.
20. Ibid., p. 62 f.

Chapter Five

1. Karl Vietor, *Goethe the Poet*. Cambridge: Harvard University Press, 1949, p. 3.

2. *Goethe* (Copenhagen, 1935–39), II, 24.
3. Ibid., p. 53.
4. Ibid., p. 60.
5. Ibid., I, p. 97.
6. A selection from Grønbech's larger work on Friedrich Schlegel was published in Copenhagen in 1949 as *Den unge Friedrich Schlegel.*
7. *Friedrich Schlegel i årene 1791–1808* (Copenhagen, 1935), p. 3.
8. Ibid., p. 4.
9. Ibid., p. 4.
10. Ibid., p. 269.

Chapter Six

1. *Jesus, Menneskesønnen* (Copenhagen, 1935), p. 18.
2. Anna Sörensen in *Svensk lärartidning* 55 (1936) No. 50, 14 Dec. 1936.
3. *Hellenismen* I, 283.
4. Ibid., p. 168.
5. Grønbech himself recognized the prolix quality of the work on Hellenism and planned to revise and shorten it for a new edition. Death cut short this plan, but the book was subsequently issued in a shortened one volume edition by his widow, Honorine Hermelin Grønbech, in 1953: *Hellenismen. Livsstemning—Verdensmagt.*
6. *Hellenismen* I, 309.
7. Ibid., 303.
8. Ibid., 171.
9. Ibid., 204.
10. Ibid., 99.
11. Ibid., 415.
12. Ibid., 420.
13. *Paulus* (Copenhagen, 1940), p. 5.
14. Ibid., p. 6.
15. Ibid., pp. 66, 87.
16. Ibid., p. 113.
17. Ibid., p. 245.
18. Review in *Berlingske Tidende* 24 August 1941.
19. *Højskolebladet* 27 June 1941.
20. *Præsteforeningens Blad* XXI (1941), 7 February 1941.

Chapter Seven

1. *Hellas* I (Copenhagen, 1942), p. 12.
2. Ibid., p. 61.
3. Ibid., p. 171.
4. *Hellas* II (Copenhagen, 1942), p. 140.
5. Ibid., p. 129.

6. *Hellas* III (Copenhagen, 1945), p. 22.
7. Ibid., p. 190.
8. Ibid., p. 24.
9. Ibid., p. 89.
10. Ibid., p. 92.
11. Ibid., p. 168.
12. Ibid., p. 96.
13. *Hellas* IV (Copenhagen, 1944), p. 52.
14. Ibid., p. 56.
15. Ibid., p. 35.
16. Ibid., p. 66.
17. Ibid., p. 109.
18. Ibid., p. 132.
19. *Lyset fra Akropolis* (Copenhagen, 1950), p. 33.
20. Ibid., p. 127.
21. Ibid., p. 126.
22. Ibid., p. 204.

Chapter Eight

1. *Kampen om mennesket*, p. 9.
2. Ibid., p. 9.
3. Ibid., p. 13.
4. Ibid., p. 13.
5. Ibid., p. 14.
6. Ibid., p. 186.
7. Ibid., p. 190.
8. Ibid., p. 197.
9. *Kampen for en ny sjæl*, p. 38.
10. Ibid., p. 117.
11. *Sprogets Musik* (Copenhagen, 1936), p. 128.
12. Ibid., p. 133.
13. Ibid., p. 31.
14. Ibid., p. 27.
15. Ibid., p. 94.
16. Ibid., p. 134.
17. Ibid., p. 170.
18. *Frie Ord* II (1947), 302–308.
19. Ibid., p. 306.
20. Ibid., p. 308.

Chapter Nine

1. *Religious Currents*, p. 16.
2. *Kampen om mennesket*, p. 9.
3. *Mystikere i Europa og Indien* I, p. 97f.

4. Ibid., p. 188.
5. *Jesus*, p. 117.
6. *Mystikere i Europa og Indien* IV, p. 235.
7. *Perspektiv* VI (1954), p. 16.
8. "Heraklit." *Vetenskaps-Societeten i Lund. Årsbok 1929*, pp. 24–44.
9. *Mystikere* III, p. 4.
10. *Hellenismen* II, p. 136.
11. *Mystikere* IV, p. 29.
12. *Oversigt over Det Kongelige danske Videnskabernes Selskabs Virksomhed Juni 1931–Maj 1932* (Copenhagen, 1932), p. 57.
13. Ibid., p. 66.
14. Ibid., p. 97.
15. Ibid., p. 113.
16. Ibid.

Chapter Eleven

1. *Politiken*, 24 March 1957.
2. *Religious Currents*, p. 175.
3. Ibid., p. 169.
4. *Nationaltidende* 26 March 1930.
5. According to Professor Johannes Pedersen, who has described himself (in private conversation) as Grønbech's closest friend from about 1910 until after World War I.

Selected Bibliography

PRIMARY SOURCES

1. Major Works by Vilhelm Grønbech
Forstudier til tyrkisk lydhistorie. Copenhagen: Lehmann og Stage, 1902.
Morituri. Copenhagen: Lehmann & Stage, 1903.
The Second Danish Pamirexpedition. A Vocabulary of the Dialect of Bokhara. Edited by Vilhelm Grønbech. (Ole Olufsen, genl. ed.). Copenhagen: Gyldendal, 1905.
Lykkemand og Niding. Vor Folkeæt i Oldtiden I. Copenhagen: V. Pios Boghandel. T. Branner, 1909.
Midgård og Menneskelivet. Vor Folkeæt i Oldtiden II. Copenhagen: V. Pios Boghandel. Povl Branner, 1912.
Hellighed og Helligdom. Vor Folkeæt i Oldtiden III. Copenhagen: V. Pios Boghandel, Povl Branner, 1912.
Menneskelivet og Guderne. Vor Folkeæt i Oldtiden IV. Copenhagen: V. Pios Boghandel, Povl Branner, 1912. (New edition based on English version: *Vor folkeæt i oldtiden* I–II. Copenhagen: Gyldendal, 1955.)
Religionsskiftet i Norden. Copenhagen & Kristiania: Gyldendal, 1913.
Primitiv religion. Stockholm: P. A. Norstedt, 1915. (Augmented edition: Copenhagen: G. E. C. Gad, 1948.)
Religiøse strømninger i det nittende aarhundrede. Copenhagen: Gyldendal, 1922. (Det nittende Aarhundrede . . . , XXV.)
Indiske mystikere. Copenhagen: H. H. Thieles Bogtrykkeri, 1925. (Festskrift udgivet af Københavns Universitet i Anledning af Hans Majestæt Kongens Fødselsdag.)
Mystikere i Europa og Indien I. Copenhagen: Povl Branner, 1925. (2nd ed. 1932; 3rd ed.: *Indisk mystik.* Copenhagen: Gyldendal, 1967. Section on Buddha separately published: *Buddha.* Copenhagen: Thaning & Appel, 1952.)
Nordiska myter och sagor. Med kulturhistorisk indledning. Stockholm: Bokförlaget Natur och Kultur, 1926. (Danish edition: *Nordiske Myter og Sagn. Med kulturhistorisk Indledning.* Copenhagen: V. Pios Boghandel. Povl Branner, 1927. 2nd ed., 1941; 3rd ed. 1947; repr., 1964, 1965, 1969, 1973.)

Kampen om mennesket. Copenhagen and Oslo: Jespersen og Pios Forlag,
   1930. (2nd ed. 1943; 3rd ed. 1949.)
Mystik og Mystikere. Ed. Vilhelm Grønbech and Aage Marcus. Copenha-
   gen: Gyldendal 1930. (Gyldendal's Bibliotek, IX.)
The Culture of the Teutons I–III (in 2 volumes). London: Humphrey Milford, Oxford University Press. Copenhagen: Jespersen og Pios Forlag,
   1931. (A translation and revision of *Vor Folkeæt i Oldtiden.*)
Mystikere i Europa og Indien II. *Heraklit. Mester Eckehart. Ruysbroek.*
   Copenhagen: Povl Branner, 1932.
Mystikere i Europa og Indien III. *Teresa de Jesus.* Copenhagen: Povl Bran-
   ner, 1932.
William Blake. Kunstner, Digter, Mystiker. Copenhagen: Povl Branner,
   1933.
Mystikere i Europa og Indien IV. *Donne. Wordsworth. Herder.* Copenha-
   gen: Povl Branner, 1934.
Jesus, menneskesønnen. Copenhagen: Povl Branner, 1935. (2nd and 3rd ed.
   1935; 4th ed. 1944, repr. 1965, 1973.)
Friedrich Schlegel i årene 1791–1808. Copenhagen: Levin & Munksgaard.
   Ejnar Munksgaard, 1935 (Det Kgl. Danske Videnskabernes Selskab.
   Historisk-filologiske Meddelelser XXII.)
Goethe I–II. Copenhagen: Povl Branner, 1935–39 (Volume I republished as
   Den unge Goethe. Copenhagen: Gyldendal, 1965.)
Hellenismen I. *Mennesket* (II. *Gud*). Copenhagen: Povl Branner, 1939
   [i. e., 1940]. (Shortened version edited by Honorine Hermelin Grøn-
   bech: *Hellenismen. Livstemning—Verdensmagt.* Copenhagen: Gyl-
   dendal, 1953.)
Sejersen fra Variager. Løse blade af Variager magasin. Copenhagen: Povl
   Branner, 1940.
Kampen for en ny själ. Stockholm: Natur och Kultur, 1940. (3rd ed., 1941.)
Paulus, Jesu Kristi apostel. Copenhagen: Povl Branner, 1940.
Kristus, den opstandne frelser. Den ældste kristne menighed. Copenhagen:
   Povl Branner, 1941. (2nd ed., 1970.)
Solen har mange veje. Sange. Copenhagen: Povl Branners Forlag, 1941
   ("Privattryk"). (2nd ed., 1949.)
Hellas. Kultur og Religion I. *Adelstiden* (II. *Revolutionen;* III. *Guder og
   mennesker;* IV. *Tænkere og Tragikere*) Copenhagen: Povl Branner,
   1942–45. (2nd. ed., 1961.)
Sprogets Musik. Copenhagen: Povl Branner, 1943. (2nd ed., 1956.)
Sangen om livet og døden. Copenhagen: Povl Branner, 1944 ("Privattryk").
Vorherre på bjerget. Sange og rapsodier. Copenhagen: Povl Branner, 1944.
Madonna og gøgleren. En slags Komedie om to mennesker. Copenhagen:
   Povl Branner, 1946 ("Privattryk").
Kampen for en ny sjæl. Copenhagen: Det Danske Forlag, 1946. (2nd ed.,
   1947; 3rd ed., 1952; 4th ed., 1963.)

Dostojefski og hans Rusland. Copenhagen: Povl Branners Forlag, 1948.
Philon. Et fragment. Copenhagen: Povl Branners Forlag, 1949. (Studier fra Sprog-og Oldtidsforskning, 209.)
Spillemænd og andre folk. Tanker under prædiken af organisten ved Sebastianskirken. Copenhagen: Povl Branners Forlag, 1949 ("Privattryk").
Den unge Friedrich Schlegel. (Edited by Honorine Hermelin Grønbech.) Copenhagen: Det Danske Forlag, 1949.
Lyset fra Akropolis. Copenhagen: Gyldendal, 1950. (2nd ed., 1969.)
Angst; Religion. To foredrag. Copenhagen: Wivels Forlag, 1951.
Livet ev et fund. En bog om humor og tragedie. Copenhagen: Gyldendal, 1951.
Hellas. Kultur og religion. Supplement. [Edited by Povl Johs. Jensen.] Copenhagen: Branner & Korch, 1953.
Atombomben og andre essays. Copenhagen: Gyldendal, 1957.

2. Books by Grønbech in English.
The Culture of the Teutons I–III. (In 2 volumes.) Translated [with the aid of the author] by W. Worster. London: Humphrey Milford, Oxford University Press. Copenhagen: Jespersen og Pios Forlag, 1931.
Religious Currents in the Nineteenth Century. Translated by P. M. Mitchell and W. D. Paden. Lawrence: University of Kansas Press, 1964. (Reprinted Carbondale and Edwardsville: Southern Illinois University Press; London and Amsterdam: Feffer & Simons, Inc., 1973.)

SECONDARY SOURCES

1. Bibliography
POUL HOLST. *Vilhelm Grønbech. En bibliografi.* Copenhagen: Povl Branners Forlag, 1948.
Dansk skønlitterært Forfatterleksikon I. Copenhagen: Grønholt Pedersen, 1959.

2. Books on Grønbech
Birgit Helene Hansen. *Omkring Heretica. Vilhelm Grønbechs forfatterskab som forudsætning for Hereticas første årgang.* . . . Aarhus: Akademisk Boghandel, 1970. (2nd ed., 1972.)
Torkil Kemp. *Vilhelm Grønbech.* Copenhagen: Povl Branners Forlag, 1943.
P. M. Mitchell. *Vilhelm Grønbech. En indføring.* Copenhagen: Gyldendal, 1970.
Ejvind Riisgård. *Vilhelm Grønbechs Kulturopgør* I–II. Copenhagen: Gyldendal, 1974.

Index

Southwest WI Library System

3 9896 01015 1039

WITHDRAWN

WITHDRAWN

LTE

B
DIANA

Brown, Tina.

The Diana
  chronicles.

$29.95   06/15/2007

DATE			

Prairie du Chien
Memorial Library
125 S. Wacouta
Prairie du Chien, WI 53821

BAKER & TAYLOR